The Fundamental
Principles And Precepts of

Islamic
Government

Book No. 2 in

Iran-e Nu Literary Collection

Ahmad Jabbari, Editor

Printed under the auspices of Amir Kabir Institute
of Iranian Studies.

انجمن امیرکبیر
برای پژوهشهای ایرانی

Abolhassan Banisadr

The Fundamental
Principles And Precepts of

Islamic
Government

Translated from the Persian by

Mohammad R. Ghanoonparvar

MAZDA PUBLISHERS

P.O. BOX 136, LEXINGTON, KENTUCKY 40501, USA

ISBN: 0-939214-01-6
Library of Congress Catalog
Card No.: 81-82634

Typesetting by: Lexington Photoengraving & Printing, Lexington, Kentucky 40508.
Printed by: Colonial Press, Covington, Kentucky 41011

CONTENTS

Editor's Preface

The Iranian revolution toppled one of history's most oppressive regimes before the astonished eyes of millions of people around the world. The struggle that culminated in the 1979 revolution had its beginning in the late nineteenth century. In fact, Iran was at the vanguard of struggle against oppression and colonial transgression in Asia long before India and China. Ironically, it finished last in its victory over internal oppression and, from the events following the revolution, it appears that final victory over imperialism and socalled social-imperialism still lies a long way ahead. It would, therefore, be less than sincere to claim — as some have — that only a particular group was responsible for the revolution, or that the "seed" of the revolution was "sown" in the June 5, 1963 uprising against the Shah. The contemporary history of Iran is a clear testimony that many ideologically diverse groups and individuals played active roles to bring about the downfall of the Shah. The list of such groups and individuals is a long one.

Now, almost three years after the people's triumph, only a few objective studies of the revolution (and the role of groups and individuals who helped to bring it about) have been undertaken. The fact that the revolution is still in process (with constantly changing socio-political parameters) has rendered such studies difficult. The existing studies can be classified into three broad categories; (1) books and articles that have been published by groups in Iran who have attempted to articulate their own sectarian interests, (2) a few genuine scholarly attempts by a handful of Iranians and non-Iranians, and (3) a large body of literature by the peripatetic "Iran experts" who, although caught by the revolutionary surprise and having to make last minute adjustments in their ongoing research, have managed to jump on the band wagon. With the Pahlavi elite and pseudointellectuals fleeing headlong during the revolution and taking refuge in various western institutions, and with a new breed of apologists emerging, there is a need for an organization to provide a forum for the expression of scientific ideas. Mazda Publishers hopes to provide this forum.

Our objectives at Mazda Publishers are to recognize and analyse the problems faced by Iran, and to attempt to provide solutions that might help to bring about an improvement in the socio-economic and political conditions commensurate with Iranian culture and tradition. This is an enormous task. A step in this direction is to introduce and study the ideological and philosophical outlooks of prominent individuals who have been instrumental in bringing about the revolution. This book is presented with such an objective in mind.*

In the future, original works will be published in the fields of arts, humanities, social sciences, and science and technology. We welcome manuscripts by all those scholars who are driven by a sense of scientific inquiry about the problems facing Iran—internal as well as relative to the rest of the world—and with a feeling of responsibility and sincerity towards the Iranian people.

*Two other works are currently underway at Mazda Publishers: (1) the biography of the late Dr. Mohammad Mosaddeq, and (2) a critical assessment of selected historical speeches of Ayatollah Khomeini.

Translator's Introduction

With the Iranian Revolution of 1978-79 and its impact throughout the world, a new impetus has been given to a general desire to understand Islam, and particularly Islam as it is practiced in Iran, or at least Islam as an ideological basis for the leaders of this Revolution. In the West, and particularly in the United States, this impact is evident in the preoccupation with Shi'ite Islam of both scholars and experts and the new-found interest of the media and consequently the general public in the subject.

Traditionally, Western knowledge of Islam has focused almost exclusively on Sunni Islam, predominant throughout the Islamic world. But even this knowledge of Islam, as Edward Said shows in his recent book *Orientalism,* has presented the average Westerner with a stereotypical view of Moslems, their society, their customs, and their religion and has consistently been coupled with a sense of exoticism (or as Said calls it, "otherness") and even prejudice.

The new "discovery" by the West, especially the American mass media, that there are different branches of Islam and that Iranians belong to a minority branch called Shi'ism took seemingly everyone by surprise. The figure of Ayatollah Khomeini as the leader of the Revolution, appearing on television screens nightly dressed in a strange, dark garb and an exotic, black turban, along with out-of-context quotations and misquotations or mistranslations of his statements, has facilitated the conclusion by the surprised Western media and the public that the Iranian Revolution is a movement opposing "modernization" and a regression to some unexplained, vague, medieval social system.

It would be unfair to suggest, however, that no attempt has been made, especially since the Revolution, to explain more accurately recent events by those who have a better understanding and a more thorough knowledge, and at times a more or less sympathetic approach to the study of Iran, Iranians, Shi'ism, and the new sociopolitical system in that country. In fact, a number of recent scholarly books and articles have shed some light on the subject.

But, still, the greatest part of the printed material available to the English reader consists of secondhand sources of information. And although a small body of works of contemporary Iranian thinkers and writers who have influenced the course of events (such as those of 'Ali Shari'ati) have appeared in translation, there remains a felt need for more sources in English.

As the first president of the Islamic Republic of Iran, elected with a decisive majority, and as a most active member of the anti-Pahlavi movement during most of his adult life, Abolhassan Banisadr has become a distinguished figure of the Iranian Revolution. With his roots and early training in a family of religious scholars, and his later education in Iran and France, Banisadr belongs to a class of scholars, like Shari'ati, who seem to appeal to both the intelligentsia and religious scholars, as well as to a significant portion of the general public. Obviously, an essay by Banisadr, especially one dealing with his vision of an Islamic government, aside from its importance for an understanding of Iranian society today, should serve as one of the historical and intellectual social documents of twentieth century Iran. Thus, the motivation for the English translation of *The Fundamental Principles and Precepts of Islamic Government* has been at least partly due to the importance of this work as a sociohistorical document.

A Note on Translation and Transliteration

A translation, by definition, is an interpretation, but it is one in which the translator should, to this translator's point of view, attempt to interfere as little as possible, remaining a conduit, so to speak. Because of the nature of this work, which was presented in lecture form in the spring of 1974 and later transcribed from tapes and published by the Muslem Student Associations of Europe and the United States and Canada, the Persian text is relatively unedited and there are the inevitable repetitions, ambiguities, and inadequacies generally encountered in lectures. The translator has made a conscientious attempt not to edit the text for repetitions, lack of coherence of argument, digressions, etc. This should facilitate for the reader insight into Banisadr's personality and thought processes, not only through his line of argument, but also from his tone, which this translation has attempted to preserve. For the sake of clarification, however, and based on Banisadr's own arguments, certain terms have been translated so as to avoid confusing the English reader. For instance, *'adl* (justice) and *'edalat* (the practice of justice) are used by Banisadr interchangeably and, hence, both have been rendered as "Justice." *Nobovvat* (prophethood) and *be'that* (mission of the Prophet) are also used as synonyms and are translated as "Spiritual Mission" since, as Banisadr argues, the concept, to him, means the Prophet's spiritual mission which continues to be the duty of every Moslem. *Be'that-e da'emi,* however, has been translated as "Continual Spiritual Mission." Furthermore, common English translations of certain terms, including the five fundamental principles, are not employed; instead, these terms have been rendered into English in accordance with Banisadr's own understanding and interpretation of them.

It must be noted here that, following the Revolution, an expanded edition of this work was published in a book entitled *Osule Rahnema va Zabetehha-ye Hokumat-e Eslami* (The Guiding Principles and Precepts of Islamic Government). No fundamental changes have been made in the new edition, and, at times, this text has been consulted for clarification.

The transliteration of Persian and Arabic words from the Arabic script follows Nasser Sharify's recommended system found in *Cataloging of Persian Works* (Chicago: AmericanLibrary Association, 1959) with minor alterations: (1) no diacritical marks are used to distinguish between various consonants which are pronounced alike in Persian although represented by different letters or over the vowel, i, (2) the apostrophe (') is used to represent the sign *hamzeh,* and (3) the turned comma (') is used to represent the letter *'eyn.*

The Roman and Arabic numerals bracketed in the text refer to the chapters and verses of the Qur'an respectively and follow those of *A. Yusaf 'Ali's* translation of *The Holy Qur'an,* 2nd ed.(n.p.: American Trust Publications, 1977). In the Persian text of Banisadr's essay, verse quotations from the Qur'an are given at the end of the book in Persian translation, but have not been included in this translation. Banisadr's translation of the verses are, however, found in the translator's footnotes whenever they differ significantly from those found in *The Holy Qur'an.* Italicized footnotes are Banisadr's own, and the others are the translator's.

University of Virginia
Fall 1980

The Fundamental
Principles And Precepts of

Islamic
Government

Preface

In an atmosphere of pressure and strangulation, in an atmosphere of continual self-centeredness, the Islamic scientific methodology for thought and action was abandoned. The fundamental Islamic principles were emptied of their content. The progressive methodology based on Monotheistic Unity *(towhid)* was abandoned and replaced by stagnant Aristotelian logic and methodology. This deviation brought about others. Under the pressure of the government of autocrats, Spiritual Leadership *(emamat)* and Justice *(edalat),* which mean a continual struggle to establish an Islamic government, were abandoned. The practice of devine science *(ejtahad),* finding solutions to our problems in accordance with the fundamental principles of Islam and implementing the teachings of the Qur'an, became enslaved in abstraction.[1]

However, a generation arose from the stormy crisis and determined not to continue the silence of the past few centuries. It rebelled against Weststruckness,[2] which had overtaken the Moslem peoples since the second century a.h. (eighth century a.d.), and began a creative uprising.

The future belongs to this generation which is building it. To build this future, it is necessary to devise a general social system. Young Moslems have begun a creative effort to put forth such a system: they have determined to break the silence and to be creative and innovative in all areas. The following discussion was presented to a gathering held to study the aspects of Islamic government. It took form through the active participation of all.

This is only a first step. The next steps will be taken more swiftly and more completely.

NOTES

1. Although *towhid* has traditionally been translated as the "oneness of God" or "monotheism," Banisadr, as his discussion indicates, does not so narrowly confine the term; thus, it has been translated in this text as Monotheistic Unity, which, as the reader will most likely deduce from Banisadr's arguments, signifies not only the oneness of God but the unity of all things and their movement toward the ultimate goal, God. Briefly, based on Banisadr's following discussion, the other four principles may be defined as follows: Spiritual Mission, man's continual duty to achieve this goal; Spiritual Leadership, providing through its energy the impetus for movement; Justice, a code of behavior; and the Point of Return, the time and place of the ultimate achievement of the goal of Monotheistic Unity.

   These terms are capitalized throughout the text to call attention to their specialized usage in this context.

   Translations of Qur'anic verses, unless otherwise indicated, follow A. Yusuf Ali's The Holy Qur'an, 2nd ed. (n.p.): American Trust Publications, 1977).

2. Weststruckness *(gharbzadegi):* a term popularized by - *Jalal Al-e Ahmad* in an influential article by the same name, published in 1962. The word has also been translated as "Westtoxication" and "Westomania," among others, and generally signifies infatuation with the West. See Michael C. Hillmann's Introduction to John K. Newton's translation of *Jalal Al-e Ahmad's* The School Principal (Minneapolis and Chicago: Bibliotheca Islamica, 1974).

1

Introduction

First of all, since our society is the result of the thoughts, actions, and struggles carried out throughout Islamic history, mention must be made of those who have protected the tradition of struggle by thinking, writing, and spilling their blood. Indeed, in our own time there have been and still are those who have led the way through their thoughts, pens, or blood. And it is on the basis of their noble efforts that a generation is presently confronting its historical responsibilities. We must remember those who have protected this tradition of struggle with their thoughts, pens, and blood. Let us set aside for now the mention of very distant personalities and their struggles and call to mind our contemporaries who have written, spoken, and then been, or will be, tortured or killed. Let us call to mind those who may not have been in prisons and torture chambers, but who have dedicated their lives to paving the revolutionary path which will surely lead to our freedom and that of mankind.

All those who work and suffer in these calamitous times are worthy of the highest esteem. We praise them all: all the champions of liberty who were tortured and who lost their lives in prisons, and those champions of liberty who have been executed, who have returned to God saying, "There is no god but God." We greet Khomeini, who became the dam-breaker and idol-breaker of our time, and Sa'idi, Taleqani, Bazargan, and Shari'ati, among others, as well as all of you, and those who in-

1

tend to pave the way for future generations. Greetings, praise, and blessings upon all the strugglers. I do not praise them, or you, because they are infallibly perfect, but because they have discarded all such notions of themselves in addition to discarding those "absolute truths" which had been fixed in their minds, and in doing so, they have become free.

By freeing themselves, they have contributed to our freedom and have given us the opportunity to reflect upon the present and future. Those questions which are being raised today could never have been raised if not for a series of discussions having created the opportunity of bringing them to our minds.

When a generation poses a problem, it also raises a question: What must be done? The mere fact that one has raised a question indicates that a thick curtain of ambiguity has been pulled aside from the eyes of one's wisdom, so to speak. Before a question has been raised, it cannot be answered. An unposed problem has no solution. And those who have raised the questions of our time have not only provided us with the opportunity to find solutions within the framework of a sound ideology, but they have also given the opportunity to all the people of our country to resist the propaganda whose goal it is to make them believe the deceptive notion that there is nothing left in Islam on which to base the establishment of a government for a modern society, and in doing so to demand the establishment of an Islamic government.

We all know that up until a few years ago it was said—and it is still sometimes being said—that Islam is no longer viable as a training ground for revolutionary human beings. It was believed that some other ideology, some other program, some other solution must be found in order to create these revolutionary beings who would create a revolutionary Iran. The foundation of the revolutionary movement was set on the Fifteenth of *Khordad* (5 June 1963),[1] and it was from that day onward that this movement was nurtured in and arose from the lap of Islam. Today our generation, decisively confronting great responsibilities, demands the establishment of a revolutionary society. Our hope and the hope of our nation is for just such a society.

My second point concerns the discussion at hand. My praise and appreciation of these people whom I have mentioned as those who not only have rescued a generation from destruction, but also have set that generation on the path of spiritual leadership and made pioneers of them, should not suggest that they are infallibly perfect. I mean to imply neither that we not allow criticism and correction of their opinions, nor that what I am saying here is the first and last word, which you must accept as divine revelation. No, that is not it at all. We can comment on the ideas of others not to reject them, but to build on them. But in our attempts to avoid thinking of persons or ideas as infallibly perfect, we must not fall into the trap of thinking that everything is relative—like what I have to say to you today—and, therefore, to be dismissed regardless of its truth. No, that would be going overboard, creating a crutch for ourselves. Following a philosophy of relativism and activism is like walking a tightrope as thin as a hair. A jolt of carelessness will tumble you into a hell, on one side, in which you have made yourself a tool in the hands of others or, on the other, in which you are an activist on behalf of your own self-interests. But we must cross this "bridge" to reach our goal, taking care not to fall off on either side of it.

On the whole, at any rate, what I am about to tell you here sums up my outlook to date.

Do not think for a moment that everything will be accomplished with lightning speed, especially given the fact that we have just left behind us this interim period during which the issue of Islamic government has been totally out of the realm of discussion; during the past few centuries, it has not been considered an appropriate subject for discussion. Only Mr. Na'ini,[2] during the Constitutional period, and Mr. Khomeini, in our own time, have dealt with the issue.

Third, since the confrontation of beliefs and opinions must focus on content, when an issue is raised here, it will not be dealt with in terms of form. The game of form and content has been played throughout history, and ruling powers have always replaced form for content, bridling movements from their inceptions within the frameworks of mere form. I will talk of the present and future and our responsibilities toward them, and if I occasionally refer back to history, I will not look at matters of the distant past which have not persisted, but at those phenomena and realities that are actual issues at the present time. The method that I will use in description, analysis, and understanding is based upon general precepts and principles that are applicable to all phenomena and current issues. This subject will be taken up another time as a methodology for thinking correctly and acquiring the ability for comprehensive understanding.

If we recognize the practice of Monotheistic Unity and the methodological search for a shared empirical recognition as the purpose of this discussion, and not the setting up of battlefronts against each other, we will have returned to the revolutionary scholarly tradition and Islamic educational methodology, and we will obtain results. Let us return to the methodology which was, and still is, practiced in our mosques and old schools and throw away the methodology that we have learned from the West, which is that one person talks and others merely listen. Let us abandon this method which has turned us into a generation of ideology consumers. Let us place the greatest emphasis on the teaching of discipline and comprehensive knowledge, that is, knowledge based on Monotheistic Unity. Thought, understanding, discovery, and acquiring a system of and the machinery for them are the keys to the City of Knowledge. Therefore, we must value them greatly. And the participants in discussion must equip themselves with a perfect system and flawless machinery.

Finally, we are not the results of any reaction to any outside group or institution. We share one method and one outlook with which we will confront the issues. We must use our own institutions to find solutions to our problems. We must not become reactionaries to events, for if we become reactionaries, we will be condemned to defeat forever and ever.

No one has ever seen victorious reactionaries. Why are they condemned to defeat? Because no system accomplishes anything without a goal. Every power acts in order to create reactions, and each reaction weakens all the more the strength and the power of those who oppose it. There are two ways to confront the problem of the strength of the self-serving demonic power. First, one can ignore it, saying "This troublesome power is here and I cannot confront it" or, "Since I cannot be free of its pursuant domination, I had better separate myself from others and lie in a corner somewhere until the present situation comes to an end." But, the departure of the passive sufferer from society when it is not a *hejrat* (that is, to consolidate forces in order to return and change the society) is not productive. The story of *Ashab-e Kahf* (The Seven

Sleepers of Ephesus) teaches us that if we want to fight against a dominating, self-serving, troublesome power, we must remain in the society and create forces to overthrow that power.[3] If, on the other hand, we leave the society and go off to sleep in a cave, when we return, even the currency may have changed and the person in power might have died, but the demonic power itself will not have been destroyed. Take, for example, the coins of Naser al-Din Shah;[4] they are no longer accepted in the bazaar, but only the coin has changed; money is still in use. The name has been changed to *"Shahanshah Ariyamehr,"* but nothing else has changed.

The second way to fight the power is to remain a part of the society. That is to say, if we hope to create a force within the society, the very foundation of our thoughts must be formed from that society. In other words, we must understand the external, internal, biological, and other problems and circumstances of that society. Then, with this kind of understanding, we can bring about a new order.

The first path or method—where one drops out of the fight in order not to be corrupted—is the path most of us have taken and are even still taking. Those who have chosen to live in the West say, "That place (Iran) is no place to live; we will live here, and when things have changed, we will return to serve our country." But when they return to the country, there is no country left. Fathers have gone, relatives have gone, children have grown up and recognize no one. In fact, even the environment is no longer the same and they are unable to recognize it. They are strangers. They cannot help but return abroad; but they remain strangers here as well, and they are destroyed by it.

Now, let us look at the second path, the path that has proved victorious for all who have taken it throughout the course of history. This is the path that Mohammad took when the two great powers, Iran and Rome, were preoccupied with each other, the path that 'Ali followed when the dominant Arab power in the guise of Islam was busy forcing itself upon the region.[5] This is the path that Ja'far ebn Mohammad took during the power struggle between the Umayyads and Abbassids.[6] This course is the course that we should follow. This is the course that every revolution has followed. What is the fundamental principle of this course? It is that forces should be created patiently but with steadfastness in the struggle, without despair, through thought and action. The true method of Islam and Mohammad dictates that one must endure a long, hard creative struggle. Revolutionary struggle differs from struggle based on fleeting desires and slogan shouting. Revolutionary work is hard work. It requires nerves of steel, great ability, and constant warring with abstractions. Abstractions force us to draw attention to ourselves. But a revolutionary should not be an exhibitionist. He must first destroy in himself any sense of ostentatiousness in order to become free, in order to act.

In any case, when we want to decide upon the best method, instead of looking back at how Mohammad acted, we should ask ourselves what Mohammad would do if he were here today. In other words, we must confront the issues by seeking help from the system of "comprehensive understanding" which the Prophet possessed. In this way, instead of looking at what he did, we look at what he would do if he were here. And the problem will be solved sooner.

According to the Qur'an (Sura Rome [XXX]), Mohammad was confronted with two powers. The Romans fought the Iranians, and the Iranians were victorious. Qur'anic verse prophesied that in a few years Rome would be victorious. In our own time, it is no different. For example, Russia and the United States wrestle, and one of them will be victorious. The next time they wrestle, the other will be victorious. What is the course we must follow against these two powers? One group suggests that we recognize the situation and be realistic. They say, "The United States is the dominant power today and Russia has accepted the Western value system, in fact their value systems are identical, the rest is unimportant". Saying that "the foundation is different" or "the essentials are different" is just empty talk; when value systems become identical, the principal ideologies gradually become alike; thus, one must stick to the West. And they have. They have formed Freemasonries, and they rule our country. But this is only one outlook. Another group repudiates the former, saying, "this is capitalism, reactionism — or whatever else — and we must stick to the power which has left this stage behind, the power which can satisfy even its intellectuals." And they attach themselves to the Russians. This is a continuing historical phenomenon.

In Iran during the period of the Abbassid-Fatemid wars, there were factions within the country which aligned themselves with these two powers; for example, there were *Esma'ilis* who sided with the Fatemids and *Seljuqs* who supported the Abbassids, and these two groups fought the Abbassid-Fatemid war with each other.[7] This is nothing new in Iran; but, of course, neither is it old. It has rather been a recurring issue. Power always attracts; it attracts some and it repels others. There are also those who believe that these two superpowers are both alike, and they believe that there is another power emerging which is virtually flawless. Later, they will find out that this new one is as rotten as the others and they will begin to lament as if the world has come to an end. What calamity do you think has come to pass? Look to yourselves. What is wrong with you that you must always attach yourselves to one thing or another? They used to say the same kinds of things to the Prophet. One group which was on the side of Rome said, "The power of Rome is no joke. With a few barefooted Arabs you will not be able to accomplish anything. The power of Rome is three-million strong; that is, it has an army several times the population of Arabia. Do not begin to daydream." This was what one group said. And the other group, who was supposedly impressed by the power of Iran, said, "If you could only see Ctesiphon, you would give up this idea. Those soldiers with their golden javelins and strange looking swords and helmets. . ." And this was true. When the Persian army would spread out in the fields, it looked as if the fields were carpeted with gold. All the soldiers were covered in gold from the tops of their heads to the hooves of their horses. When the sun shone on the Sassanian army, the golden helmets, javelins, and other implements of war glittering in the sun created an awesome sight. They used to ask the Prophet, "Do you hope to fight such great powers with this handful of naked Arabs?" These were the advocates of "positive neutrality," or as Modarres calls it, "status quo neutrality,"[8]

But another policy exists which is known today as "passive neutrality" and which Modarres terms "negative equilibrium." He explains that negative equilibrium is the basis of our religion. I am not the first to have raised this issue. It was also noted by that great man of history, who in our contemporary Iran, his religious standing aside, is an unmatched social personality, a truly strong man with strength of vision.[9] And he is correct. In fact, this issue does not originate with him, but is brought up in Sura Rome of the Qur'an, wherein God says:

given the opportunity, when two powers are at war, you should expend your efforts in trying to become powerful yourselves and not in trying to stick to one power or the other; you must take advantage of the opportunity, for tomorrow will be too late.

During the period when there was the same kind of conflict going on in Iran, we took the opportunity and created the circumstances which resulted in the Oil Movement.[10] But we did not take the opportunity to make these circumstances permanent. The Prophet, on the other hand, took the opportunity and did not get involved in the quarrel between Rome and Iran. He never involved himself in the war, for example,to send a message to one of the two parties offering to bring the Moslems to their aid, or to send a message to the other side that if they gave him this or that concession, he would support them. He did nothing of the sort, let alone latch on to them. He did not do so because he had not yet become a power, a major force. One only jumps in the ring when one has become powerful. The Prophet later took the opportunity to become a power.

So, this is one kind of policy. I think those who have faith in themselves will recognize this path to be the one that time and history have proven right. We must never lose the opportunity to become powerful and independent by letting ourselves be the pawns of one power or another, as we did in our own time during the years between 1960 and 1963, when we became the pawns in games and a whole generation was destroyed as a result.

Now, to conclude these introductory remarks, in order for an individual to avoid making himself out to be infallibly perfect, in order for him to believe in himself, that is, to come to know himself, his role, and the environment in which he plays that role, in order to attain this belief in himself, a minimum of awareness is required. After all, an individual should only speak within the limits of his own awareness. Although I have thought about the role of an Islamic form of government in the world, I have not thought in definite terms about how such a government might be implemented. I have thought about Iran's position as a part of the world community at the present time, about Iran's economic, political, cultural, and social position as part of the world community. Because my theoretical outlook is one based on Monotheitic Unity, I do not separate Iran from the rest of the world as structuralists do; I do not study it as an isolated phenomenon.

My research method is not a Marxist one; that is, I do not divide history into periods. I deal with history as a current in which continually existing issues are in a conflict of cause and effect.

I do not think of conflict as something inherent and internal, but, rather, as incidental. I consider the relationship between social classes a result of alienation from one's true nature, a constant reality in various forms worldwide. It is with these notions in mind that I speak to you, and in general terms, not in detail, because if we decide to talk in detail, we would necessarily talk for three or four consecutive days. For example, if we should suggest a program of foreign trade for an Islamic government, we should not be expected to specify details, the position of everyone of the customs officers. Brothers and sisters, not that what must be clarified is the general framework; in fact, even the general framework is not very important. Instead, a scientific method should be found; then, each of us will be able to contribute to building a part of the whole in accordance with our different fields of expertise.

Since I will document what I say with the Qur'an, you must know what I understand by the language of the Qur'an. As you know, the Qur'an repeatedly states that its language is lucid Arabic, a language which is *gheyr-a zi 'evaj*, that is, it contains no distortions. Well, now, based on my methodology, I would like to pose a question: What is meant by the language of the Qur'an being lucid Arabic? Does it mean that Arabic is a lucid language and other languages are not as transparent as Arabic? This is one way to look at it. If a question is posed in this manner, the answer would be, "Yes, Arabic is a lucid language; it conveys meanings precisely; expression in this language is devoid of any ambiguity," But there is another approach to the issue. We can ask, "Does the clarity of this language suggest that the passage of time will not make it ambiguous or lessen the credibility of its content?" As a matter of fact, the language is so lucid that even now, fourteen centuries after they descended from Heaven, the verses carry the same meaning as they did then. This is what is meant by lucid language. If the language of the Qur'an were one whose meaning would change at every period of history and with every society, that is, if it spoke of issues that existed only before and during the time of their descension, and not at present, it would not be lucid language. We could not then understand the meaning of the language and the verses. But, since it speaks of what was happening then as well as today, it is lucid language and there is no ambiguity in it.

Thus, the language of the Qur'an is the language of continuing phenomena and realities.[11] For instance, if we want to understand the meaning of *al rejal-o qavamun-a ala-nesa'* (men are pillars for women), an easy but mistaken way would be to define the words as they exist, saying that man has always had absolute dominance over woman and still has; therefore, Islam endorses and prescribes this domination. So, *qavamun* - means *mosalatun* (dominant). And what a dominance! How could one accept that God — Who, not wanting such dominance over His creations, gave them freedom of will — could have made man the absolute ruler over woman? The problem with and the objection that may be raised against such an interpretation and analysis of the verse becomes obvious when we understand the phenomenon of the relationship between man and woman. Until we understand the phenomenon, we cannot understand what the Qur'an says. Thus, when it is said that the language of the Qur'an is lucid, this does not mean that as soon as you consider an issue in the Qur'an you can say, "Very well, since the language is lucid, we must call up a translator to translate it word for word." And then the translator, who knows nothing about the issue, translates the verse as "men are dominant over women." "Well," adversaries of Islam might say, "The issue is clear; how can one be more reactionary than this! You say yourselves that the language is lucid, and this language clearly states that man is the master and woman the slavemaid."

But, such interpretation will not suffice. We must understand the phenomena and the real issues contained in each verse. Taking this into consideration, the language is lucid and explicit. Thus, we realize that in certain affairs men and in certain other affairs women are, separately, but mutually, the guardian pillars *(qavamun)* of the family as a social unit based on Monotheistic Unity.

NOTES

1. Fifteenth of Khordad: a day of uprisings inspired by religious leaders, particularly Ayatollah Ruhollah Khomeini who was subsequently exiled to Iraq.

2. Mohammad Hoseyn Nai'ini,(d. 1936): a leading clergyman and activist during the Iranian Constitutional Revolution of 1906-11.

3. *Ashab-e Kahf* (The Seven Sleepers of Ephesus or The Companions of the Cave): Qur'anic story (Sura XVIII) of several companions who slept for an extended period of time, although they thought it had been no more than a day.

4. Naser al-Din Shah: Qajar King, reigned 1848-96.

5. 'Ali ebn Abitaleb: Fourth Caliph of Sunni Moslems, considered by Shi'ites as the immediate successor to Mohammad, hence, their first imam.

6. Ja'far ebn Mohammad, or Ja'far Sadeq: Sixth imam of Shi'ite Moslems. Umayyads (661-750): First Moslem dynasty, founded by Mo'aviyeh, to rule the empire of the Caliphate, overthrown by the Abbassids (750-1258), who claimed descent from Mohammad's uncle, Abbas.

7. The Fatemids were a North African Moslem dynasty which ruled that region (909-1171) and tried, without much success, to challenge the Abbassid rule of the Islamic world. (See note, above.) The Seljuqs were a dynasty of Turkic peoples who ruled Iran during the eleventh century. The Esma'ilis were a sect of Shi'ites most active as a religiopolitical movement in the ninth to thirteenth centuries.

8. "Positive neutrality" and "status quo neutrality" are translations from the Persian *movazeneh-ye mosbat* and *movazeneh-ye vojudi,* respectively. And, "passive neutrality" and "negative equilibrium," following, are renderings of *movazeneh-ye manfi* and *movazeneh-ye 'adami,* respectively.

    Seyyed Hasan Modarres, (d. 1939): a leader of the clerical block in the Iranian Parliament and staunch opponent of Reza Khan, later Reza Shah (see note 7 in Chapter 2) in the early 1920s.

9. References to either Dr. Mohammad Mosaddeq, or Ayatollah Khomeini.

10. Reference to the nationalization of the oil industry in Iran in the early 1950s.

11. *Let us consider ourselves. We are continuing realities, as are societies. The Qur'an does not concern itself with incidental issues, those which apply only to a specific time, whether a short or long period of history, those which may not occur again. If this were the case, that is, if the Qur'an only related the phenomena and affairs of the first century A.H. (seventh century A.D.), it would be no more than an antiquated, useless book now. By way of example, the Qur'an prohibits usury. Usury is a continual social and economic issue. If it were an incidental issue, the Qur'anic verse concerning usury would no longer convey a message. All right, so it is forbidden. Now, you might ask, "What if we eliminate all that is forbidden, have we not, in this case, discredited all the parts of the Qur'an which deal with these things?" No, not at all. Then we will have acted upon that part of the Qur'an. We will have eliminated them from the life of mankind and we will have advanced along the path of Monotheistic Unity. And if we act accordingly upon all the directives of the Qur'an and can claim like 'Ali in Saffeyn, "I am the manifestation of the Qur'an," the supreme society of Monotheistic Unity will have been realized.*

2

The Fundamental Principles of Islamic Government

Now, let us begin with fundamental principles, a research methodology, and the understanding of reality. Here, again, I must make an introductory remark, which is that I will not indulge in philosophical arguments. Some of those who have gathered here and who are familiar with philosophical questions might think to themselves that the issues I am discussing are philosophical ones. That might be; but, that does not concern me. I will not try to prove the existence of God; I will, rather, explain a system, an apparatus, and with it begin my inquiry. Thus, in talking about the principles of Monotheistic Unity, rather than trying to prove the existence of God, I will deal with all the dimensions of the principle of Monotheistic Unity. I will elaborate on what I have said in *"Az Moharram ta Moharram"* (From Moharram to Moharram) and *"Be'that-e Da'emi"* (The Continual Spiritual Mission) and on what our other brothers, such as Shari'ati, have talked about.

My job is not to deal with those philosophical arguments which became prevalent during the Abbassid era, especially by Ma'mun, arguments that robbed the fundamental principles of religion of their content. My task is to investigate Monotheistic Unity as one principle, as the basis of the other four principles, which all together comprise a system, an institution, that can guide us in resolving every problem and can guide us to comprehend fully in our search for solutions as well

13

as protect us from error.[2] The principle of Monotheistic Unity, the basis or foundation of the other four, combined with the others, constitutes a system that can answer any question you might have.

For instance, if you ask what marriage is, the system will provide you the means to understand the characteristics of an Islamic marriage. Should someone speak of the characteristics of marriage, or anything else for that matter, you must first comprehend it methodologically. You must understand the actual issues; then, with the help of the above-mentioned apparatus, you must try to see whether the matter at hand is an Islamic institution or not. When you truly understand the actual issues, you will see that Islamic institutions follow these five principles. If the characteristics you are given do not follow these principles, they have obviously been falsely attributed to one of the imams.

An Islamic government, a congregation based on Monotheistic Unity, can only materialize when everyone of its members becomes a spiritual struggler and religious scholar *(mojtahed)*, when no one needs to ask another what he must do, because such would result in a religious dictatorship. Since in an ideal society everyone would be a spiritual struggler and religious scholar, the Qu'ran must have foreseen this; God, the founder of Islam, must have prepared the way for all human beings to comfortably and easily equip themselves with an intellectual system which will readily facilitate thinking. As Imam Ja'far Sadeq has said, the fundamental principles must be presented to the people to enable them to understand the issues.[3] And if we equip ourselves with an understanding of those principles, we will immediately understand what the design of an Islamic government is all about.

With this introduction in mind, let us now take a closer look at these five principles.

Monotheistic Unity

The first principle, the basic principle, is Monotheistic Unity *(towhid)*. Before discussing how a harmonious system made up of these five principles is formed, I must explain the motion of Monotheistic Unity. To begin with, Monotheistic Unity does not modify, it acts. It is not a state, it is a motion. And as motion, it requires directive principles, the other four principles, which will prevent this motion from deviating from its direction and goal. We must find reflections of all the other principles in each of the five principles. Continual Spiritual Mission *(be'that)* cannot be clearly meaningful without Monotheistic Unity, Spiritual Leadership *(emamat),* Justice *('edalat),* and the Point of Return *(me'ad).* Islam is not conformity. The religion of Continual Spiritual Mission is found in a system which is constantly evolving (Suras IX, 33, and LXI, 9). That system is the Qur'an. Spiritual Leadership is leadership on the course of Monotheistic Unity with Justice as its guideline, that is, trying to reach the Point of Return, the ultimate manifestation of Monotheistic Unity.

If we view Continual Spiritual Mission apart from the other principles, we become perplexed. Continual Spiritual Mission and motion always exist, but so do the forces of dualism, as in class-structured societies. Only this system of leadership, direction, and finally motion and mission will distinguish the Islamic spiritual mission from other movements (Suras XXX, 30; XXXII, 24; XXVIII, 41; and IV, 76). But the basic principle is Monotheistic Unity. The other four principles merely express and explain the motion of Monotheistic Unity. As such, we agree with those who say that we do not have more than one principle, Monotheistic Unity. But, as we recognize Monotheistic Unity as a motion rather than a state, we consider the other four principles as those which express and distinguish the motion of Monotheistic Unity and regulate human movement. These four together with Monotheistic Unity constitute the five fundamental principles of the system.[4] We consider these five principles (each of which must be recognized and understood in the light of the others), in relation with one another, as the fundamental Islamic system for the practice of divine science and the movement of Monotheistic Unity. And it must be noted that, in analyzing, we search for the relationship between actual events and continuing phenomena.

Monotheistic Unity can be understood in two ways. First, we can go back to history citing that fourteen centuries ago, in the Arabian peninsula, idols were worshipped; there was dualism; there was trinitarianism, and so on. Monotheistic Unity means saying "no" to all that, saying "no" to polytheism and atheism. At the same time, we tell ourselves that the language of the Qur'an is the language of continuing phenomena, and while there were dualism and trinitarianism in those days, they do not exist now; therefore, the discussion is superfluous and irrelevant to the present situation.

The second approach to understanding Monotheistic Unity is to consider it relevant to the present situation, that is, to try to see how Monotheistic Unity relates to the present time. In order for individuals to be transformed, to become revolutionaries, they must change in two ways: outwardly and inwardly. There is no first or second. Mental change affects a change in action and when action changes, the mind also follows suit. They influence each other and drive one onward. Thus, if we say first or second, it does not mean that the first must absolutely happen first followed by the other. No, they happen simultaneously, which is the way to look at things through Monotheistic Unity. We believe that every action produces an effect, which in turn will produce another effect. And mankind will be set on the correct path, that of Monotheistic Unity, as a result of constant revisions of actions and views. Thus, change must take place in the matters of the mind to enable man's thought structure to change.

Correspondingly, the exterior must also change and influence the matters of the mind. For instance, in the case of the revolution of Khomeini, in addition to having triggered certain external accomplishments, it has been and will be the cause of great changes in the minds and the thought structure of the masses.[5] Thus, Monotheistic Unity has two aspects, one internal and the other external, concerning actual events in the society. We speak of internal and external matters, but this does not mean that they should be considered as totally separate. They are interreleated, as are, for example, the sun and the mountains on which the sun shines, allowing the mountain to be seen.

We will investigate these two aspects in two parts, A and B:

A. Monotheistic Unity as the great mental revolution, the greatest revolution in human thought, fighting gods and their fabrication. In this part, we will look at five issues: (1) fighting against the principle of polytheism and manifestations of gods, against the agents of discrimination of any kind and the ideas of racial, national, tribal, familial, and, in today's terms, class superiority (Sura XII, 38-40); (2) fighting against dualism and trinitarianism as the bases for the amassment of power in one or more centers (Sura IV, 171); (3) fighting against the cult of personality, which concentrates power in one center and promotes a human being to the status of an autocrat and not to that godliness — after all, God is not autocratic (Suras XXVIII, 4, and X, 83); (4) fighting against dualism, which manifests itself as an agent of God (Sura II, 79-80), or considers God an autocrat (Sura VI, 148) and man His partner in this autocracy, or makes oneself or another person out to be infallibly perfect; and (5) purging the definition and the concept of monotheism by fighting against the concept of a single God as a combination of opposites, such as justice and tyranny, knowledge and ignorance, autocracy and indifferene.

B. Monotheistic Unity as embodying the actual movement of the society towards an ultimate society of Monotheistic Unity: (1) man's freedom from all real and imaginary fetters and shackles, from bigotry and discrimination and (2) a discussion on relativism, absolutism, and the Point of Return, or the era of the creation of a definite and irreversible society of Monotheistic Unity.

The conclusion of A and B: Monotheistic Unity is the basis for a system of study and a methodology for recognizing reality, which follow the manner that God Himself has used to deal with internal and external gods, idols, etc.

Now, let me explain in detail the above-mentioned topics.

Monotheistic Unity as the Great Mental Revolution

Fighting against Gods and Their Fabrication

The primary function of the principle of Monotheistic Unity is the destruction of thought structures based on dualism, fighting against the principles of polytheism and the manifestation of gods and against the agents of discrimination of any kind, including the ideas of racial, tribal, and familial superiority.

It is said that if you sleep for three days without dreaming you will die. Dreams play a very important role in regulating the workings of the mind and the life of human beings. Sociologists say, "If a society has no myths and does not create them, it too will die." Rostam is an Iranian myth.[6] The present regime is mythologizing Reza Khan.[7] They bombard you from left and right with all that the "founder" of modern Iran did. But sociologists also say that the duty of a prophet is to break myths. Why? What is the function of a myth? It functions to tie the society to its past so that it will not progress.

For example, the Arab tribes used to record their family trees — who is whose offspring — and everyone kept such a record of his own family. What does this signify? It signifies that the future will always follow the past. The Arabs' idols manifested their social structure. Today's idols are not Lat or 'Ozza or that other one who was made of dates that were eaten when the worshippers were hungry.[8] Instead, today we have all these statues that fill the streets. His Great Imperial Majesty and so forth. The function of a prophet is to break idols, to break the dependence on the past in order to set humankind in motion toward the future. Thus, the first function of Monotheistic Unity is to destroy myths.

But you may ask, "How can a society live without myths?" It is true that myths have manifestations which are either external, appearing as idols and statues, or they are internal. You can see now why sculpture has been so strictly forbidden by Islam. A reactionary society cannot survive without the myths of a reactionary regime. And these myths appear in material and nonmaterial forms. This phenomenon is a continual one; only nowadays there are no idols hanging in the Kaaba, although in the old days there were both kinds of idols, the hanging Seven Poems (mental myths) and also physical myths.[9] The Prophet is called an iconoclast because he destroyed both kinds of myths. But this was not all he did. Myths exist and affect the individual and the society internally and externally, spiritually and physically. Our appearance, our countenance, reflects the dominant myths of our social life. When our society does not reflect Monotheistic Unity in its countenance, we can infer that dualism has nested in our spirits and the human being has been culturally dominated by another; internally, he is in conflict with his own emotions. If he is to begin to sruggle, he must first destroy this conflict within himself, that is, he must enlighten himself. Then his countenance will correspond to what is within. If he does not do so, his spirit will eventually follow suit with what is without. Thus, fighting against idols and myths, both imaginary and concerete, is not a simple task.

But, it is an important one, the most important of tasks. We see that from Abraham to Mohammad, from Mohammad to Khomeini, idols have constantly been broken; yet, idols still govern. And in military courts and government institutions, we see inscribed: God, Shah, Country. "Shah" is centered on the top, below to one side is "God", with "Country" on the other. In addition, that commander-in-chief (the miserable Ariyana[10] says, "Of course, in our time we cannot live without an ideology. We must advocate monarchism, more specifically, that the shah is God on earth."

When we consider the cult of personality and the myths of this cult, we will see how the principle of Monotheistic Unity has been used to fight against this cult.[11]

In our own time, the most common myths that dominate our world are those of science,[12] progress, power, change, and so on. Personalities, as they represent science, progress, power, etc., are superhumanized and superdeified. Personalities have been turned into idols, with their manifestations evident in every aspect of social life. It is through these very myths that a ruling regime succeeds in transforming people or breaking and destroying them under the great, unbearable weight of its stagnant system. These myths create an accumulation of power at higher levels and isolation and disunity at lower levels, among the masses. And the energy of the society is turned against itself.

Thus, he who follows the path of Monotheistic Unity must break, in the manner of Mohammad, all the myths of reactionism, these models of dualism in human behavior, any instrument in any shape or form which robs mankind of life and motion. Praise to him (Mohammad) who was the greatest iconoclast of history, and to Abraham before him and others after him, even to our own time (Sura XXI, 51-52, 58). We must break these myths in order to destroy the existing dualistic value systems and create a mental predisposition for human freedom.

Fighting against Dualism and Trinitarianism,
Which are Bases for the Amassment of Power
in One or More Centers

As the situation stands, dualism and trinitarianism have been created by economic and political powers and intellects

19

having accumulated at the poles of power — as in today's world, where economic powers, thinking powers, that is, knowledge (centers for mental activity), and political powers have all accumulated at these poles.[13] The principles of trinitarianism and dualism at the time of the Prophet's mission consisted of the two worlds of good and evil. The world of evil or the world of the "other" was the world of the enemy. And their own world and their own people, so they believed, were the chosen ones, who had been given the mission by God to guide all human kind. And they still make the same claim (Sura V, 20).[14] In any case, in those days, the world was divided into good and evil, and today it is divided into devleoped and underdeveloped! And who is the leader? The developed world!

Nowadays they talk about the dual or the triple poles of power. That is, now the world is conceived of as having three centers of power in which forces amass, and regulating the affairs of the world means managing the relationships among these three powers. This state of affairs creates an impression on the mind, produces symbols, produces gods and myths. This type of relationship between powers requires myths and symbols. These manifestations represent the trinitarianism of our time. And this matter is a continuing reality. It can be seen in every institution, every system, every regime, everywhere. This continuing phenomenon has existed since the distant past.

In the West, they call it, in its new form, the spiritual world and the material world: Spiritual affairs come under the domain of religion (in capitalist societies, some spiritual matters come under the domain of the church), which must take care of church and "spirituality," and material affairs come under the domain of government. The bottom line is that the priest's function is to merely go to the church to hear confessions. And even there, his main duty is to make certain that the system is not disrupted, since if it should be disrupted, the church would lose control of spiritual matters, too, and then, even the confessional would be disrupted!

These are all interrelated. But in the beginning of Iranian mythological history, there were no classes. Everyone lived like everyone else.[15] Jamshid appeared on the scene and divided the society into classes.[16] Up to that time, nonpolitical leadership was given to religious powers, whose duty it was to manage only social affairs — like the moderator, whose duty is confined to keeping order in a meeting and regulating exchanges of opinion; he is not a superpower with a bludgeon to hit us on the head. Yet, they say that if he, the moderator, remains in that position for a long time, under the right conditions, gradually these powers will begin to amass in him and, willingly or unwillingly, he will no longer remain our representative. He will, rather, become the representative of the very power accumulated in him. Then, through him, this power will dominate us. This may be called alienation from social duty and social leadership, or, in our terminology, leadership through a political ruling power or government.

Jamshid was just such a person in whom power amassed and made him its representative, to such an extent that he even claimed to be God. In the section on the Cult of Personality, I will return to the story of Jamshid, who divided society into three distinct parts. This is a characteristic of the social structure of Iran, which classifies the society on a political basis. Even today in Iran, such classifications are based on the accumulation of political power and not on economics. Jamshid, too, divided the society on a political basis. He said, "Let the clergy go to the mountains; there they are closer to God." He expelled them from the society and sent them to the mountains. And he divided the rest of the society into two groups: those who produced, whose duty it was to produce agricultural and industrial products, and those whose duty it was to fight or manage the affairs of the government, that is, the class of statesmen and soldiers—the dualism of the powerful and the laborers. This dualism has created both abstract and concrete myths.

The dualism of that period is also forming in our country today: They say religion is separate from politics. This idea is itself based on the dualism which is said to be the basis and foundation of the present day social order. Political power is concentrated in a center consisting of the army and the government. (The government accumulates political, financial, and economic power within the society.) This power claims that there are two worlds, the spiritual world and the material world, that there is a great gulf between them, that they are not related at all, that the clergy should just keep itself occupied in the mosque and not stick its nose where it does not belong.[17] In effect, they tell the clergy, "Don't bother with what Abuzar or anyone else did; this would be sticking your

nose in where it does not belong.[18] Stay where you are and per-
suade the people to obey his majesty. Give thanks that the state
is "safe and secure." Do not make a move. This is your duty.
If—God forbid—people should take up arms, you should say,
"It is a crime; heaven forbid; I take refuge unto God." This is
the only duty of the mosque. More than this would be sticking
your nose in where it does not belong. If you carry out your duty well, our "sire" will be able to do his work comfortably.

So, the phenomenon remains; only its myths have changed. They used to say that the world has essentially two gods,
the god of good and the god of evil. Now they say that there are
essentially two worlds, capitalism and socialism—not as
systems, these are merely guises for Russia and America. You
must compromise with either one or the other. There is no
other choice! The myths are capitalism, on the one hand, and
the proletariat, on the other (poor proletariat!). In one place,
the manifestation is Nixon and in the other, Kosygin. This is
what we must destroy.

Having convictions is not the same as idolizing this or that
power. As Mosaddeq said in response to the Tudehs after
September, 1941, "There is a difference between conviction
and dependence.[19] It is one thing to have the conviction to support the workers, it is another to blindly obey. Conviction does
not nessitate blind obedience (as Mosaddeq told Pishehvari[20]).
Conviction does not necessitate blind obedience.
So you claim that you support the workers. What does this have
to do with taking orders from the Soviet Union? For what
reason do you take orders? Because you consider the Russian
government as the absolute representative of the working
classes and believe it must be obeyed. That is all. All I can say
is, you are in Iran, belong to it! Support the working classes
and we will welcome you. But, as soon as you begin to regard
Russia as infallibly perfect, you are saying that to support the
workers means to say that Stalin, the wise leader, did this, that,
or the other, and therefore you must follow him unquestioningly. Then, when he dies, you start writing letters of repen-
tance and self-reprisal for having followed him, blaming it all
on the personality cult. And then you start all over again. You
find another one and make a "religion" out of worshipping
him. And we will wait and see whether you begin self-reprisals
after the death of this next one as well, saying that he, too, was
part of a cult of personality.

But, what is the basic problem? The basic problem is that, each time an idea has become a "form" and the "form" has become a "myth," it has become an opiate of the masses and the instrument of oppression. Andre Gide, the French poet and writer, made an interesting comment. He was a communist who went to Russia, but returned only to resign from the Communist Party. This is what he says:

"We worked so hard to drive God out of human life and we thought we were rid of Him for good. I went to Moscow and I realized that, well, at least you don't have to look at the Christian God day in and day out; however, there, God is a very visible ten-meter-high statue, every one of his fingers one meter long, the statue of Lenin! I realized that I could not refuse to accept this god, for every time I opened my mouth, if I had changed one iota of what they had said, they accused me of being anti-Marxist and anti-Leninist. This god really has become an awful bludgeon. Even the Communists themselves threaten each other with it."[21]

Thus, we do not need to return to distant history to explain dualism. We will try to show the continuity of the phenomenon, the present reality, and we will try to explain how, in today's world, these power myths have divided up the world and have crippled humanity. They say there is no other way, that we must choose either to become dependent upon Russia or America, that anything else is merely self-deception! They say anything else is unscientific, unrealistic, illusory, belonging to the world of imagination.

Fighting Against the Cult of Personality

This is not a cult in which, as you might think, all assemble to choose one individual as their leader and god to then worship—like Hitler in Germany, Stalin in Russia, de Gaulle in France, etc.—or in which, as you might suppose, we want to sanctify and worship Mosaddeq, Khomeini, or other personalities, or even the imams and the prophets. Until a human being has accepted Monotheistic Unity as an all-encompassing struggle against dualism, he will not understand this point. The following verse is found in several chapters of the Qur'an: "I am human, like you." The Prophet repeatedly says that he is

23

no more priviliged than you are, except that he receives divine revelation.

"I am human, like you." Why should he say this? Because he is afraid that an Othman, a Mo'aviyeh, or a Mansur will mythologize him, use him as a bludgeon against the poeple and deprive them of their livelihood.[23] Furthermore, the Prophet was a great man. He could not be an advocate of dualism. If he were to represent himself as infallibly perfect, he would not be an advocate of Monotheistic Unity. He would be an advocate of himself (Sura III, 79). That is why he has carried out the most stringent fight against the Cult of Personality in the course of history and has not made of himself an exception.

There are those who oppose the Cult of Personality, but only for others. They see their leader as an excpetion. Mythologizing Chairman Mao, picturing his head as a sun which brightens up the world, if this is not the cult of Personality — considering a human being as infallibly perfect, his eating habits the best of all, his sleeping habits without-match — then what is it? They believe that one should not deviate a hair's breadth from his words, and if one thinks or expresses thoughts other than his, one's head must be chopped off. We ourselves also have a form of this kind of myth: the shah, "his majesty," as the ultimate master of all sciences. You ask, "of economics?" Oh, yes, his majesty had expressed views which have astounded economists throughout the world; in fact, of the five or six great personalities of the world, his majesty is one of two through whose dexterity the world goes 'round, and so on!

One of the functions of the Prophet of Islam was to fight against those who make absolutes of themselves. Thinking of oneself as infallibly perfect is a disease which, when it progresses, qualifies one for an insane asylum. In one's imagination, one can think of oneself as a Napoleon setting up an army, invading, and conquering. But the Cult of Personality is a social issue. It reflects a social structure, a structure based on the Cult of Personality from the very top to the lowest stratum of society. Even education is "based" on the Cult of Personality.

Concentration of power in one center means that the society has accepted such a structure, that powers must be amassed in certain centers which must be "worshipped" in one way or another; power and force are "worshipped" as values, in one manner or another. Otherwise, the society cannot remain tranquil and be tamed, it will not tolerate this amassment of power. No one, unless he supposes the amassment of power in power centers to be natural, will accept being a slave to power.

Hence, the Cult of Personality is the by-product of both the subjective and the objective worlds, which are born of one another, together creating structures by which the dynamic forces of the society are amassed in certain centers. Those forces are rendered ineffective or are used to maintain the status quo when harnessed and concentrated in centers outside the society. The Cult of Personality is, in fact, the cult of power. Therefore, an attack on the Cult of Perosnality is not only an attack on his majesty, not only an attack on Hitler, not only an attack on Stalin, as idols, but it is essentially a genuine attack on the social structure and system which have produced such figures. It is an attack on the regime that allows whoever sits in the seat of power to become an absolute ruler, regardless of whether or not this is his desire, even if he declares ten times daily that he is not a god. The reason 'Ali ebn Abitaleb did not participate in the power play on the day of *Saqifeh* was that he would either be forced to become a god, the god of tyrants, or he would be killed before he could establish the foundation for a long-term movement and a struggle in the general course of history.[24] Today, the Cult of Personality is the cult of power. It is a world-wide cult, one found everywhere. If power is concentrated in the person of an individual, he will be worshipped.

In our own time, power is worshipped in the form of symbols, idols, and signs everywhere. Absolutism must be crushed everywhere and man freed of it. Monotheistic Unity means fighting against the Cult of Personality: *La ellah,* there is no god...as we have seen, in the Cult of Personality, there is talk of worshipping absolute power. Autocracy is worshipped. Note that the Hitler worshipped as a symbol is not a symbol of God (because God is not an autocrat) but, rather, a by-product of the social structure and the blind manifestation of power. If power is not absolute and people are not allowed to do whatever they want, power can never amass in the person of one individual no matter what he says or what he does (e.g., one day proclaiming a "white revolution" and the next day a "yellow" one).

The principle of Monotheistic Unity requires the absence of any economic, political, intellectual, or other centers in which power can be amassed. Therefore, those personalities mentioned above are not manifestations of God; they are manifestations of Satan.

The administration of the society will follow the course of Justice unless social institutions are molded into forms which obstruct movement. Their becoming rigid forms results in a disruption of functions. One institution, for example, ultimately takes over the functions of other institutions, forcing itself upon them and replacing their very foundations. That institution has, since the beginning of history, been political, the ruling power which operates on the principle of autocracy. That is why the function of the Minsitry of Education is to propagate the worship of absolute power, symbolized by myths. hence, a teacher must train the youth in such a manner that they become accustomed to accepting and tolerating abosolute power.

So, when you open a first-grade textbook, in accordance with this principle, you find a picture of the Shah on the first page. There is no mention of God, all is "His Imperial Majesty, So-and-so," and the like. A few pages later, you find a picture of the Empress, and still a few pages later, that of the Crown Prince. Such an educational institution is based upon the praise and worship of autocratic power. And it is according to this principle, this "superior value," that the children of the country are educated. The youth of the country are trained in such a manner that they consider blind power as the only value, as completely natural. They become so alienated from themselves that they imagine autocracy to be ideal. Do not think for a moment that such propaganda, such education, is ineffective. They fill the mind of the child with the worship of power. Later on, they might change the myth, but dualism and the worship of power will remain. Look around you, you will see that you have been unaware of how deeply the wound has been inflicted. The economic institutions, the economic structure, the programs are all focused on and set up to facilitate the amassment of wealth and profit in power centers.

But, what of the rligious institutions? A religion corps is to be established. *Hoseyniyeh Ershad* and mosques are to be closed.[25] Why? Because religion, too, must be regimented to propagate autocratic power and not to struggle against it. As a result, the upcoming generation loves autocratic power; it will obey its superiors, and if it ever attains a position of power, it will expect absolute obedience. Such an environment, such a system, produces automatons; it works exactly like a machine that takes in raw material from one end and emits a finished product from the other. This machine, the society, takes in human beings, who are by nature free, and emits people who are self-centered and obedient to autocracy. Islam fights against the Cult of Personality, against autocratic power, and against self-centeredness.

The Islamic system, which is founded upon free principles, five general, fundamental principles constant and present in all phenomena and their interrelations, produces human beings. Such things as prayer, fasting, pilgrimage, and holy struggle *(jahad)* are continual exercises that help one return to one's own nature. Islam is a continual cultural revolution changing dualism into Monotheistic Unity, changing a dualistic person into a monotheist so that he can see himself in others and others and the world in himself. The effects of centuries of living under dualistic conditions, thought and action based on dualism, cannot be destroyed, except with the continual exercise of Monotheistic Unity, of thought and action based on Monotheistic Unity. This is the true meaning of the Islamic form of worship.

In conclusion, the fight against the Cult of Personality is the fight against the social system which propagates it. What is being criticized and fought against is the social regime. Islam does not intend to quarrel one by one with the few lunatics who ride the backs of the people. It, rather, confronts the "pharaoh" as a myth, as the product of a social regime. Hence, the regime is the target. There are more than seventy verses in the Qur'an concerning the pharaoh and the pharaoh-producing system — of course, even if today's pharaohs are not called pharaohs, their behavior is pharaoh-like — so that you and I will know that there is a pharaoh in each of us. Do not think that it is only the Shah who considers himself the infallibly perfect knower of all things; you and I, too, do the same, because we have been reared under the same educational institution, with the same dualistic "religion." We all worship our own personalities. That is why we are unable to unite.

The Cult of Personality is the deadliest of narcotics and the greatest obstacle confronting the society and Monotheistic Unity. Unless we fight against the cult, we will not be free, we will not be able to come together in one assembly, we will not be able to find a common identity, and we will not be able to become a liberating force. We must fight with decisiveness and urgency against the environment and the foundation of dualism.

Fighting Against Dualism

The fourth problem is fighting against dualism as regards the power of the Almighty. As we have seen, when the society is based upon blind power and autocracy, the symptoms are evil. Such autocracy overpowers the human being and spreads like a cancer from the depths of his soul to his very countenance. Everyone is an autocrat in his own way and in proportion to his own power. One who considers himself infallibly perfect would not submit to anything but power; that is why we hear, "We people deserve tyranny." Look at an army, any army. It follows this model precisely. A low-ranking officer must obey his superior blindly and unquestioningly. The principle in operation here is that autocratic power is sacred and must be obeyed. The central power is the chief commander, the "Commander-in-Chief," the source of fear and hope. Oh, what foul dualism! Even the downtrodden—those who obey and bear the insufferable burden of the dualistic system, who work all their lives only to see what they produce with their life's labor amassed in autocratic power centers—when they attain power within this social system with the same thought structure which is the product of dualism, unfortunately, transform into dominating powers themselves. Why? Because their value system is that very dualistic value system and their power is based on autocracy. So, power rapidly alienates them from themselves, transforming them into a dominating class. Such has been the tragedy in all human societies throughout history.

Nothing is more of an enemy to human beings than unsound ideas. Unsound ideas are an enemy with which human beings become impassioned to the point of destruction. To become united, we must continually fight against and shatter these kinds of ideas, this structure which belongs to a system based on autocracy. We must continually ask ourselves, "Is this view I have formed the last word on the subject?" One should not stretch back comfortably, as one would after having eaten a big lunch, and say, "Ah, those views which I have formulated so well are the beginning and the end." No! No! One must search, one must question, one must confront the issue, one must present his views and discover what shortcomings they contain. With this approach, one may find the way to progress, to change, to evolve, to become a spiritual leader, and to work for his freedom and that of others.

Ideas which have become absolutes are the enemy of human freedom. These thoughts exist in the depths of one's being. But they are the foundation of dualism. They are the last thing to leave a person's mind. And since they are based on autocracy, it will take a long time before these symptoms are destroyed and the mind is freed; before this structure is destroyed and another structure based on Monotheistic Unity replaces it; before a monotheistic pioneering human being moves towards Monotheistic Unity, on the path of Justice, under the Islamic system, reaching Monotheistic Unity at the Point of Return; before a time is reached when mental and physical absolutes are eliminated forever.

In any case, this is not the only characteristic of mental dualism. Another facet, which is one of the important afflictions of our society, is that one considers an instinct or desire (sexual instincts, the desire for comfort, the desire for delicious food, the tendency for exhibitionism, etc.) as absolute. The human being who is the product of an educational system based on dualism is an impotent plaything of these instincts and desires. Today, based on the weakness and impetance of mankind, which lives within the dualistic system, policies of systematized tyranny (the army, police, prisons, torture, etc.), education, and propaganda are formed and carried out. It is on the basis of such dualistic thinking that the ruling class plans and carries out its investments and production programs. The motivating forces manipulate the alienating mechanisms of the individual's overriding tendencies to obstruct human freedom: The dynamic mental forces, the products of creative minds, the dynamic forces produced through the labor of the society, etc., are taken from the society and used to prevent it from becoming free. Men and women are alienated from themselves through the manipulation of their sexual and other desires, and their political, economic, social, and cultural behavior is bridled and directed as the dominators see fit.

Whether or not you are an economist, you can clearly see that an important part of the Western economy operates on "sexuality," which dominates production and consumption. The industrialist says, "If we conform production to actual consumption and to actual human needs — considering, for instance, that human beings need sleep, food, and protection from heat and cold — and base production on these needs alone, it will not be long before the surplus of capital will create a crisis; since the market will overflow with goods which fulfill these needs, soon the unused capital will creat a crisis and will endanger the existing system throughout the world; therefore, if we are to maintain the economic status quo, we must regulate production so as never to flood the market." He considers which human instinct will never be satisfied. Sex. A person may be sexually stimulated at any given moment. You can make a person addicted to continual sexual stimulation. Addiction to sex is the most powerful of addictions. Heroin addiction and other addictions cannot even come close. Using sex, you can force such an addict to consume a product; even food, even a mattress, a quilt, or a heater can be sexy.[26] They tell you, 'If you wear these clothes, you will look sexier; if you behave in this or that manner, your sex appeal will increase a hundred-fold."

Therefore, one of the foundations of systems which operate on the principle of the amassment of power is sexual energy and attraction. From childhood on, the primary value, the highest of values, consists of the combination of wealth and sex. Hence, as soon as the child becomes aware of himself, he begins to pursue these two. He directs his every movement and all his energy along the fastest course which will lead to these two.

What a confinement for free human action: Man is free to sell and destroy his mental and physical energies. This is nothing new. In ancient Babylon, just like today's Paris and London, sex was one of the fundamental regulating factors in political, economic, and social relations. This is part of the class system in which every means must be used to employ the dynamic forces along a course which serves the ruling power.

We have spoken of the economic aspects, but more important is the aspect of anger. Anger represents the will for change, the will which is particular to a people who have suffered privation. This is a dynamic force which can transform the society. If we do not neutralize it or alienate it from ourselves, it can set the society on the path to freedom. Since the 1868 rebellion in France, "houses of love" have increased by 60 percent, and in Iran, the atmosphere has become heavy with sex and drugs. And that is how the dynamic   force of a generation, the generation's will for change, has been guided into a swamp of social and cultural decomposition.

Among the characteristics of dualism is a desire for superiority through wealth. In the Qur'an, we read the story of two friends, one of whom becomes the owner of a garden. His garden bears fruit. He tells his friend, "I am financially superior to you and since I have more, I have taken a more beautiful wife and I have more beatuiful children as a result." In this manner, he considers himself more distinguished and superior to his friend. He is so wrapped up in himslef that he even begins to boast before God. He says, "Who is God? While I am here, He is nobody," Dualism ends in heathenism. His friend says, "Before you owned the garden and had an income, we were believers in God, we were friends. But since you have become the owner of a garden, you refuse to answer my hello. Worse than that, you deny God. Are you not afraid that God will take it all away from you?" He answers, "What God?" As you see, in spite of what is said, the continuing reality is that the accumulation of wealth brings with it heathenism. God says, "Of course the belongings of that dualist were taken away" (Sura XVIII, 32-42).

As soon as you consider personal wealth as the ultimate goal, you are practicing dualism. In this vein, absolute possession is one of the characteristics of laws in the West, whose legal system is based on dualism and individualism. Islam, on the other hand, only recognizes one type of possession, that gained through work and effort within the confines of the five fundamental principles, and nothing else.

I have explained the mental aspects of dualism, the economic aspects, and the instinctual and psychological ones. Further explanation of other aspects of mental dualism is necessary, but since time does not permit, I will not indulge in such here.

Fighting against the Concept of God
as a Being Possessing Contradictory Characteristics
such as Justice, Tyranny, and Despotism

So far, we have talked about those dualistic bases of the

structure of the mind which the Qur'an has addressed and their relationships. Now, we will talk about the concept of a despotic God, a God of contradictions—unfortunately, we Moslems, too, understand God as such. This concept, which is the tyrannical result of the stratification of the freedom of action on the basis of degrees of power, is particular to those societies in which "freedom" of action depends on one's political and economic positions on the social ladder.

For example, the Shah has absolute power. He can do whatever he pleases. But, autocracy decreases the lower one goes on the social ladder. In such a system, the concept of God in the minds of the people reflects the status quo. After the death of the Prophet, two movements, one in support of the government and another in support of the *emamat* based on Justice—faced each other in opposition. The more the regime inclined toward autocracy, the more the concept of a contradictory, autocratic God was propagated. In the same way that man became the product of a dualistic system, a plaything of desires, and dependent upon a value system based on blind power, God, too, became a plaything of desires and a prisoner of a value system based on blind power! But the regime was ignorant of the fact that God has a different value system, which He advocates through His prophets.

In order to say that this person represents that one and is, therefore, the boss, the master must be an autocrat, so that his representative, too, can function as such. Then the problem is resolved. If one protests, they answer, "He has said it Himself." Hence, when they asked Mo'aviyeh, "Why do you do the things you do?" he answered, "It is the will of God. God Himself has said, 'I will give possession to those I choose.' If He had not wantd to, He would not have given possession to me. He has also said, 'The ways of right and wrong are in My Own hands.' If the righteous and evil paths are in His hands, who am I to argue? If I do right, 'It is in His hands' and so also if I am unjust. It has nothing to do with me" (Sura VI, 148).

Hence, in a system based on autocracy, God is considered the greatest of powers. But God is useful for one purpose alone, that is, to justify autocracy. It is not God Himself, as such, Who is used by the absolute ruling power to justfy autocracy; the main concern is power itself. God is only considered God because of His attributed absolute, blind power. Power is, in itself and by its very nature, absolutist and blind. The goal of every power is to become more powerful. Good and evil are only understood in the light of being more or less powerful. The acts of power have no other precepts but becoming more powerful and despotic. Ascribing good or bad characeristics to power shows a failure to understand it. Therefore, God is considered the absolute almighty, and He can do whatever He wants, whether just or unjust. Such a God has always had (and still has) a representative with absolute authority, called the king.

Among the mythological stories of Iran, the story of Jamshid is the story of alienated social leadership, the leadership of absolute power, an ascension (in truth, descension) toward godhood. Jamshid was said to be a person who could eliminate cold and heat, who could eliminate old age and disease, who could eliminate hunger, and so on.

Satan came to Jamshid and said, "God, who had not done any of these things, told the people to worship Him and the people obeyed. When God existed but you did not, there were such things as old age, death, heat, and cold.Since you have come, none of these things exist any longer. You are more deserving of being God than God Himself. Declare that you are God and behead anyone who refuses to accept it." He answered, "Not a bad idea." Temptation overtook him. He was no longer a representative of the people, he became a representative of power. He sent for the spiritual leaders to be brought down from the mountain. He said, "I have done away with cold and heat, and much more. Not even God has been able to do these things. Why should I not be God? Go and force the people to accept me as God. If you do not, I will have you beheaded." And it is said that Jamshid became a devious man. The result of this deviousness was foreign domination of Iran and the kingship of Zahhak.[27] Zahhak was an Arab, not an Iranian. He took over Iran and ruled for a thousand years. Why? Because Jamshid claimed to be God and deprived the people of all pride and security. Later on, in the actual history of Iran, the Shah became the representative of God. Look at the engravings which remain: the Shah receives the emblem of kingship, the ring of power, from God.[29]

In summary, when God is seen as a despot, His representative becomes a despot as well, on a different level. Such has always been and still is the justification and theoretical basis for the autocracy of heads of government. In order to clarify

33

this, to see how power alienates the human being from himself, let us consider the story of Alexander:

He set out from Greece as the liberator of the Greek regions controlled by Iran, and he arrived in Damascus. He then went further and felt the desire to be the son of God. In Egypt, he went to a temple, made a sacrifice, and gave bribes (so-called offerings) to the temple and the spiritual leaders. The chief of those liars, that is, those disguised in the garb of the intellectual and ideological leadership of the society, working to justify the actions of the blind power and the deterministic domination of the ruling class, called Alexander the "son of Jupiter."

By the time this son of God had arrived in Hamadan, he had declared himself to be God. "I am God Himself," he said. "I am not the mere consequence of the copulation between my father and mother; I was born of the union between God and my mother. I am the son of God and it is my right to be a god." One of his commanders came forth and said, "When you left Greece, you said you were a liberator. In Egypt, you became the son of God. Here you are Jupiter. What will you be when you reach India?"

In our own time, when someone becomes a symbol of a social system and the mythologized figure of an ideology, he claims, "Ideology means I; opposition to me means opposition to Marxism-Leninism; opposition to me means opposition to the Iranian monarchy; opposition to me means opposition to religious law'" an so on. In Iran, since after fourteen centuries of awareness of Monotheistic Unity, it is difficult for the people to accept that he (the Shah) is the son of God, he dreams that the Prophet, the imam—'Ali or Mehdi, or someone else comes to him to discuss the next day's agenda[30] And he is allowed to do whatever he pleases.[31]

You can see that the continuing reality still holds. It comes in various shapes, but it still persists. Therefore, the struggle to destroy the foundation and the system that make dualists and heathens must continue. The system and the tools for fabricating gods must be destroyed. The idea of a despotic God must not be accepted, in order to prevent the appearance of a despotic representative of Him. Doing so would serve to cleanse and purify the definition of God to bring it in line with Monotheistic Unity, which is one of the most significant and noble functions of Islam. The God of Islam is not a despotic

God, because despotism signifies weakness and weakness is not deserving of God. God is not an accumulation of contradictions; He is pure Justice. Since this will be discussed extensively in the section on the continual Spiritual Mission, this much will suffice for here.

Fighting the Material Foundations of Dualism

Monotheistic Unity as the Negation of Divisions

In my articles *"Az Moharram ta Moharram"* (From Moharram to Moharram) and *"Be'that-e Da'emi"* (The Continual Spiritual Mission), the guiding principle for anlaysis is that Monotheistic Unity is motion and not a state; hence, monotheistically unified movement within the system is made possible. This system does not come to be merely through the connection of its various components. The essential element of the system is the creation of a dynamic force. The motivating force *(emamat)* drives the movement forward on a course as follows:

The system is a dynamic amalgamation in which elements — themselves amalgamations — are predisposed to join together, to work together in search of Monotheistic Unity.[32] The components combine according to specific proportions, acting and reacting together. Each functions in relation to the others. Together they make up a force that provides the system with a directed movement.

If the elements are perfectly combined, that is, if there are no elements in the system that also belong to other systems and there is no predisposition to combine with the elements of any other system, the system will be complete, stable, and self-sufficient in its own natural environment, and it will continue its singular identity.

Now, let us consider human society as a system. If the dynamic forces created in the society are amassed in certain centers through divisions such as class, race, or nation, the system will fall out of line with Monotheistic Unity, and the ability of the elements to combine will suffer. A good example would be Iran from ancient times up to today. As social, racial, national, and other divisions solidified, the amassment of active forces and wealth in centers of power increased. When the

Safavids came to power, they had nothing. Many of the soldiers of Shah Esmaʻil's army had no swords. But by the end of Shah Soltan Hoseyn's regin, everyone was covered in gold from head to toe.[33]

If the dynamic forces do not amass in centers of power, that is, if there are no divisions to instigate the amassment of forces, whatever the society produces will create greater forces proportionate to the degree of Monotheistic Unity. Under the influence of the dynamic forces, the society will move more rapidly towards Monotheistic Unity, which will, in turn, intensify the dynamic forces. This mechanism is that of independence, the mechanism of Monotheistic Unity: When the dynamic forces work toward a singular identity and toward increasing the speed of the movement of the society in this direction, the society will, in turn, increase the dynamic forces as a result of the increase in the degree of Monotheistic Unity. But, if there are divisions, the opposite will occur. For instance, if a country makes $1 billion, of which $800 million is spent within the society and the remaining $200 million is taken out of the economy, and it is not actively invested in the economy of the society, no change will occur in that society. But, if that $200 million is invested in the society, more minds and bodies will begin to operate and production will increase. Suppose that the result of this increase in production raises the surplus from $200 million to $300 million. Obviously, when this motivating force is employed, more minds and bodies can be put to use. In this event, the society will change.

The kind and direction of change and the destiny of the society depend on how these and other motivating forces are used, and the way they are used depends on these social divisions. When divisions exist, inequality intensifies, and the society rapidly dissolves into conflicting forces. But, if there are no divisions—on neither a national nor an international scale—Monotheistic Unity and unification will be within reach. The Point of Return indicates where and when Monotheistic Unity will materialize. In this case, the forces will be directed toward infinity, and the divisions that exist in the world today, such as nation, race, and class, will be eliminated forever. If we operate within the framework and eliminate these divisions daily, we will create a worldwide society based on Monotheistic Unity.

Now we realize that if we remove the creation of the dynamic   force from a specific system, there will no longer remain a system, that is, it will become a dead system whose elements have lost their function and relationship with one another, and have lost their united identity, and been dispersed into multiple identities. We say that our world as a system is not a harmonious whole, therefore, it is not a society based on Monotheistic Unity and it profligates its great resources. Those centers of amassed power attract all the financial, mental, physical, and other talents to themselves and leave behind an impotent, dispersed world suffering from tyranny. Those centers deprive the rest of humanity of thinking as well as producing and using the produced energies, the motivating forces it has created.

Monotheistic Unity means removing the dividing lines and liberating human beings from strict, Stone Age forms, forms which have disabled the human being, prevented his movement, and robbed him of the energy to move, condemning him, as a result, to foul decomposition.

Now that we have seen that Monotheistic Unity is movement whose goal is the elimination of dividing lines and forms, we must find out what the social motivating force of this movement is. What is the force that causes change, and how can it be recognized? The Qur'an says (Sura XXVIII, 5): "I have willed that the downtrodden laborers be the inheritors of the earth."[34] What does "inheritors" mean? Is this succession a simple one? Does it signify that the exploited, downtrodden, and mistreated will gain power and then, in turn, mistreat and exploit; that this is the way of the world; that each will take his turn? If this is succession, there will be no change in the system, the same old system will remain, and life will go on as before.

If the succession of the downtrodden in place of the powerful — the demonic powers and pharaohs — means that the laborer will take the place of the ruler, become a ruler himself, and operate within the very same value system of the dualistic society of pharoahs, there will be no fundamental change in the society. Once again, a minority will rule, a majority will constitute the downtrodden, and God's promise will have been one of those same old empty promises.

The downtrodden will only become true inheritors when the bases of dualism, class distinction, and discrimination are destroyed in the society and in the mind, and are replaced by

Monotheistic Unity, when a new value system — the Islamic value system based on Monotheistic Unity — replaces the existing one. Let us return to the Qur'ran to see whether this is truly so and whether Islam has established the foundation of Monotheistic Unity. Is Monotheistic Unity a basis for solutions? Are the dividing lines eliminated in Islam? Does Islam accept discrimination? The Qur'an says:

> ...We created
> You from a single (pair)
> Of a male and a female,
> And made you into
> Nations and tribes, that
> Ye may know each other
> (Not that ye may despise
> each other). Verily
> The most honoured of you
> In the sight of God
> Is (he who is) the most
> Righteous of you (Sura XLIX, 13).

Values follow piety, that is, movement along the path of Justice, on the path of relativism and activism, within the framework of the Islamic system, toward Monotheistic Unity. This is the great value of Islam. The precepts of the Islamic high values (piety) are Spiritual Leadership and Justice, the training of relative, active human beings, pioneering human beings seeking Monotheistic Unity.[35]

Hence, we do not accept race as a foundation. Our principle of Monotheistic Unity opposes such a foundation. It opposes slavery and profiting from human energy spent in the interest of one class or group. We might be asked, "Then, what is this buying and selling of slaves in Islam? Is it not true that there is a chapter concerning the buying and selling of human beings in the books of religious law?"

Let us look at this phenomenon of slavery in history. We should see how slaves were taken in ancient times. And even today, during the war with Germany, those who captured the Germans forced them into some sort of slavery, both in the West and on the other side (Russia). The form has changed, but the content has not. When Darius conquered Asia Minor, he would clear a city; he would separate those with a profession or trade and bring them to Iranian cities as captives. There he would settle them so that they could work for the Iranians. The rest, he would either put to the sword or leave in their plundered city, forcing them to send him annual taxes and tributes. This was the way things were done. Whenever his majesty's treasury got low, he would plan to plunder some area or other. He would declare war, go and plunder the area, and take humans, their belongings, and whatever else he desired. Later, he would sell the spoils. This was a common practice, not only with kings. It was a common practice for someone in debt to sell or hire out his son, his wife, or himself. As you may know, Abu Moslem (and this was even after Islam) had been sold by his father to pay off his debts.[36]

Slaveholding and slave selling are continuing historical issues. Even today, the buying and selling of human beings takes place everywhere. The most common practice is to sell oneself as a worker for the duration of one's productive years in exchange for the necessities of life. Another kind of slavery in practice is importing workers under conditions worse than those of slaves of the past. For example, the government of Germany signs a contract with the government of Turkey, according to which the Turkish government is to send, let us say, 500,000 people as workers to Germany to work in German factories. Since you yourselves know why, I will not belabor the point. This is slavery. The name has changed, but the practice remains the same. This unjust system will transform human beings into slaves, worse than that, into objects.

Slavery has been and still is the destiny of the largest segment of, if not all, humanity. Islam challenges every type of this continuing reality in one way or another. As regards slaveholding, the challenge which comes to mind most readily concerns the buying and selling of human beings. First of all, Islam had to destroy slaveholding as a principle; it had to forbid the buying and selling of human beings, and it did.

The kind of slavery which exists in Islam concerns captives of war. If an Islamic army fights a heathen army—that is, if they should attack and we find it necessary to defend ourselve—they would take captives from us and we from them. When no agreement is signed between us concerning the exchange of captives, they could take our captives and sell them as slaves. Therefore, in war conditions, we have the right to buy and sell these captives. That is the extent of it (Sura XLVII, 4).[37] Since this went against the principle of Monotheistic Unity and, at the same time, the captives of war could not be abandoned, given the relationship with the enemy, Islam was bound to provide a means whereby slaves could be set free. Islam organized a persistent struggle which allows the captive-turned-slave to gradually make his way to freedom within the Islamic society.

This persistent struggle against slavery in all its forms is only possible in a perfect system. Islam has been and still is such a system, which has organized a historic struggle against human captivity.

Nation, or nationalism, is a kind of religion. The West today has made a sort of religion out of it. Nationalism is, in fact, a religion in which the assumption is made, for instance, that the French, as a national entity, have prior rights to the rest of the world. Such is the meaning of nationalism.

Hitler's nationalism claims, "The German race, even one German life, is superior in every way to all other races." If there is a conflict involving the life of one German and one hundred Indians, for example, the hundred Indians would be sacrificed to keep the German alive. This is nationalism. Nationalism does not allow our rights to be our own. But in Islam, everyone's rights are his own.

Nationalism is particular to the amassment of power on national and international scales. It is created by and accompanies at all times this amassment. But, considering one's identity and rights as one's own and someone else's as his own (passive neutrality) is an Islamic idea. Therefore, we have no quarrel with those who say: our rights belong to us. But, we do quarrel with those who believe that all rights belong to the victor—in effect, "Our rights belong to us and others' rights belong to us as well." As an Islamic nation, we do not have the prior right to use everything in the world. This is not the case. If such a meaning of nationalism and we accept nationalism as such, we are acting against the principle of Monotheistic Unity. Islam has never said that since the Prophet came from the Arabs, the Arabs are superior to the rest of humanity.[38]

In the Qur'an, there are two verses expressing the same idea, one of which I will quote. In Sura *Nahl* (XVI), Verse 71, we read:

> God has bestowed His gifts
> Of sustenance more freely on some
> Of you than on others: those
> More favoured are not going
> To throw back their gifts
> To those whom their right hands
> Possess, so as to be equal
> In that respect. Will they then
> Deny the favours of God?

The first part of the verse is contrary to Monotheistic Unity. Not that there is a word in it that conveys dominance; it mostly refers to Spiritual Leadership. But, this is the first part of the verse. When it is separated from the second, you have a case similar to that of "men are dominant over women" and it would appear that the principle of social class is acknowledged. But, we have said that in the Islamic system, movement is towards Monotheistic Unity. Class has never existed in God's value system. God did not intend to send the Prophet to ensure the continual domination of the ruling class. After all, they knew how to protect their own interests as well as how to take the belongings of others away from them. They had managed quite well up to that time, and they did not need God to send them a prophet to regulate their affairs, because they had no problem. Those with problems were the downtrodden. It was they who lived in difficulty, and still do. Ask a Marxist and he will tell you:

Yes, actually, they did have problems. The fact that you have been dominated, you are in chains, and you are a laborer has probably prepared you mentally to accept this situation as natural; otherwise, you would rise up in struggle. External conditions alone will not spark a revolution. The mental conditions of dominated classes must also change to make revolution possible. Awareness is an essential factor. It is not enough for everyone to merely be under similar conditions, as the tools of production. It is necessary for the people to become aware of themselves as a class in order to begin to move. Religion transforms the cries of revolution into "prayers" and prevents the laborers from becoming aware of themselves. When they become aware of themselves as a class, they will abandon religion as the mental facade of a class society. Hence, it was necessary for the ruling classes to express themselves through Mohammad, and consecrating and spiritualizing class dif ferences eliminated any sort of doubt, so that the dominated classes would accept their condition as the will of God: "God has bestowed His gifts of sustenance more freely on some of you than on others..."

But, the first part of the verse is incomplete without the second. With the help of a system consisting of the five fundamental principles of Islam, we find that the first part of the verse explains an undeniable continuing natural reality, and the second part explains the social solution of the problem based on the five fundamental principles. The issue mentioned in the beginning of the verse is an issue of continuing reality: In actuality, in the existing, real world, abilities are not equal. For example, one person is more powerful while another more intelligent, one is more creative while another..., and so on. This is the result of motion.

Motion is found in society and in nature. As an example, let us look at marriage. If marriages take place following the dictates of nature, that is, if the genes combine as nature dictates, the result will be natural. But in society, marriages do not take place as such. As a result of the dominance of the social aspects of marriage over the natural aspect, the offspring produced by various marriages differ in intelligence, while another is retarded. Of course, within the motion of Monotheistic Unity, where thought and action occur within the Islamic system, marriages are corrected. In the course of this movement, exceptions decrease and intelligence moves towards equality and towards Monotheistic Unity. But, there is a long way to go before we reach this goal. And, meanwhile, we cannot leave the affairs of society as they are. Something must be done; otherwise, the dominators will take over or will remain dominators, alienating themselves from themselves as well as alienating others. What is the Islamic solution?

In accordance with the fundamental principles, the solution is as follows: It is true that I with an inferior intellect, for example, cannot work as well as you with a superior one, but in proportion to the difference in our intellects, you will be able to enjoy more of the possibilities that society puts at our disposal. Therefore, if you are to employ all your talents, you need the society more than I do and you must contribute to the society by producing more. In this way, the general opportunities will increase and equality for all will ensue. You will be able to expand your intellect and will replace the dominator as a spiritual leader. The second part of the verse expresses the following concept: In partaking of this provision, you are equal to your inferior. This is the meaning of the principles of Monotheistic Unity, Spiritual Leadership, and Justice, and of the movement of Monotheistic Unity. It is true that, in a society based on Monotheistic Unity, superior and more mature intellects may exist; however, these intellects must be used as pioneers in order to prevent their transformation into a class of the intelligentsia, which, by dominating others, wastes its intellects.

Relativism and Absolutism

The movement of Monotheistic Unity is a never-ending movement. The more we progress towards Monotheistic Unity, the more the movement will increase and accelerate. When none of the energy of the movement of the entire apparatus is wasted, the apparatus will have become perpetual motion with a unified identity. No matter how far we progress in this movement, there is still a long way ahead of us. There is a long way to go before we reach pure Monotheistic Unity, before we return unto Him. Hence, no time, no era is ever the end, but always the beginning.

Relativism requires us not to think of any era or time as a state, not to consider it the absolute end of the road. Every era or time is a stage of continual motion. It is not a state. And since it is not a state, there is no stagnation; there is always speed and velocity. There is no final point in thought, in society, in nature, or in anything else. The Point of Return itself is a beginning, the beginning of the ultimate society of Monotheistic Unity, which has no refuge but God. At the Point of Return, we will have arrived at a point where there is no possibility of returning to a Cain-and-Abel society. All those factors and elements, inequalities, and dualism will have been totally eliminated, as will the road of return. Spiritual leaders are proof of God. No decree but the decree of God:

> I do call to witness
> The Resurrection Day;
> And I do call to witness
> The self-reproaching spirit:
> (Eschew Evil).

> Does man think that We
> Cannot assemble his bones?
> Nay, We are able to put
> Together in perfect order
> The very tips of his fingers.
> But man wishes to do
> Wrong (even) in the time
> In front of him.
> He questions: "When
> Is the Day of Resurrection?"
> At length, when
> The Sight is dazed,
> And the moon is
> Buried in darkness.
> And the sun and moon
> are joined together, —
> That Day will Man say:
> "Where is the refuge?"
> By no means!
> No place of safety!
> Before thy Lord (alone),
> That Day will be
> The place of rest
> (Sura LXXV, 1-12).

The Point of Return is the time when there is no refuge by Monotheistic Unity and no road to dualism and no other path but Monotheistic Unity. This is the Point of Return. In his Continual Spiritual Mission, man will free his destiny from the web of continuing realities and will return to Monotheistic Unity, return unto Him.

Hence, Islam is not absolutist, but relativistic. But it does not follow absolute relativism, thus, it recognizes a beginning and a Point of Return; it follows relativism in mission and motion. But it does not consider this mission and motion of Monotheistic Unity as temporary; it recognizes them as continual.

Movement is subject to the existence of the system, which I have already defined. Now, we can say that we cannot consider movement outside of a system. That is, before various elements in a system establish a relationship, they will not act together. Neither will they become active as a unit.

To explain this more clearly, let me bring up the following example, which is important especially to those who work with

44

their intellects. The act of thinking is the movement of thought. Thinking is impossible without a specific subject. Before a human being knows specifically where he is, precisely what his subject is, and before there is a relationship between his thoughts and his environment, he is unable to think. This is precisely the difference between fantacizing and thinking. Fantasy has no specific basis in reality. One could be sleeping quietly and, in the world of fantasy, travel the seven heavens, still remaining where he is. This is different from thinking. Elements which connect thoughts to one another must belong to that specific subject. Analysis seeks to find the relationships between realities, how they interact, and what laws govern them. In passing, let me say that the reason why the "weststruck" person cannot think is precisely because he has been cut off from his specific subject (his society and natural environment).[39]

Therefore, if a monotheistically unified movement is to take place, it must occur within a system suitable for this movement. If you work within a system based on dualism, you will certainly end up in a society in which there is all manner of class discrimination and you would be moving toward the abyss of reactionism. You will not stay on the course of relativism and activism (Sura IX, 54).

Continual Spiritual Mission

I have written previously on the Continual Spiritual Mission.[40] Here, I will repeat briefly what I have said before. Islamic prophethood offers a system based on Monotheistic Unity, a system for the return to Monotheistic Unity. In our holy book, the Qur'an, the fundamental principle and the principle elements of this system are provided for human beings, based on the concept of continuing reality, to enable them to undertake the Continual Spiritual Mission within this system, which is both a system for social Monotheistic Unity as well as a system for thought and action.

To make man's Continual Spiritual Mission possible, not only should the mental structure which is unsuited for such a persistent struggle change, but man must constantly be in a state of uprising and resistance. For this purpose, a new understanding of man is necessary. This new understanding of man, creative man, man seeking Monotheistic Unity, relative, active man, is what Islam provides. In "The Continual Spiritual Mission," I have talked in detail about this man. You, as human beings, are relativists and activists — this is the principle of Justice — only when you and your society base your efforts on neither of the two following premises:

First is autocracy as a principle, according to which man is an autocrat. One form of it in our own time — the philosophical form which deals with rights — is popularly known as "existentialism." The other premise is determinism, that is, the idea that a human being is merely an "instrument" incapable of free will, productivity, or movement. These two premises are dualistic and oppose God; they are counter to the principles of Continual Spiritual Mission and Spiritual Leadership. The principle which would become meaningful in the movement of Monotheistic Unity — that is, Continual Spiritual Mission — is related to Monotheistic Unity in that Monotheistic Unity is motion and motion is impossible without a system and the Islamic system is one in which this motion can take place. This system must free mankind completely from obstacles which obstruct movement so that man can become free-spirited in the movement of Monothiestic Unity.

Hence, these two principles are the touchstones for understanding Islam. If we come across instructions which do not agree with Montheistic Unity or which conform with immobility and stagnation, they are not Islamic and must be discarded, because Monotheistic Unity is the beginning and the end, the mission and motion towards this goal. Immobility is disharmonious with this God-willed motion.

That is why the Qur'an says: "Wherever a tyrant is found, we will choose a prophet from among the masses of the people who have not been alienated from themselves." There is always talk of motivating, but never talk of lying down to sleep. Holy Struggle (*Jahad*) is the basis for the choice: God values strugglers over resters with great rewards. Holy Struggle is a value and this value requires a basis. Every value rests on a basic principle. The basis of Holy Struggle consists of the fundamental principles of Monotheistic Unity, Continual Spiritual Mission, Spiritual leadership, and Justice. Without Holy Struggle, Continual Spiritual Mission is impossible, without Continual Spiritual Mission, Spiritual Leadership (therefore, Holy Struggle) is impossible, without Spiritual Leadership, movement on the course of Justice is impossible, and without all these, the society of Monotheistic Unity is impossible. Therefore, since the principle of Spiritual Mission is a general principle, you and all God's good people have missions, and since we all have missions, we cannot accept immobility. To change the thought structure and the social structure from dualism to Monotheistic Unity is to heighten the movement quantitatively and qualitatively. Without the Spiritual Mission, Monotheistic Unity cannot materialize.

The principle of Spiritual Mission is necessary for evaluation. For example, whenever we are told that the Islamic family is thus and so, we can immediately use the principle of spiritual Mission as a touchstone to show that it is the collective which can move and that movement takes place within a system. The individual is nothing. He is incapable of movement, because it is in the collective that you with me and I with you can establish relationships wherein our thoughts interact. The movement of thought is the result of these relationships and the interaction of views and ideologies (Sura III, 200). So, movement takes place in the collective. And God created the collective. He created a system and a collective, because he created movement, and it is in the collective that movement occurs.

To illustrate in a nutshell the relationship between the fundamental principles, God is located in infinity, and Spiritual Mission is movement within the Islamic system through Spiritual Leadership on the path of Justice (relativism and activism) towards the Point of Return at a time and place where the strongholds of dualism have all been destroyed and the unswerving movement of Monotheistic Unity will begin: Unto Him do we return.

Spiritual Leadership

We will now deal with Spiritual leadership, which is the guiding principle in establishing and organizing an Islamic government.

Spiritual Leadership, like Spiritual Mission, is a general principle. That is, all of us, if we seek Monotheistic Unity within the Islamic system, will be the pioneers of a mission of Monotheistic Unity. The Qur'an says: "Man seeks to open the way for his own progress" (Sura LXXV, 5).[41]

Man's motion, man's ingenuity, man's struggle, and those forces which motivate him are all crystallized in this desire: Man, the creature who has lost himself, longs to reach the Point of Return of becoming himself, to return unto himself. Spiritual Leadership, as a dynamic force and the will and desire to return to oneself, is hidden within every human being. The spiritual leader's function is to open the horizon, to open the road. But man's motion is constantly threatened by a tendency to change direction from Monotheistic Unity to dualism. If the system governing the society and the intellect is a dualistic one, this force and desire for return to the self will lose its way and will sink the human being into the swamp of dualism. That is how the leader of dualism and the leader of Monotheistic Unity differ. The spiritual leader of Monotheistic Unity is the symbol of motion, the dynamic force, and the will to return to the self within the Islamic system.

The second characteristic of Spiritual Leadership is that the spiritual leader has no ties with race, class, or group. The active Spiritual Leadership of Monotheistic Unity is the force and the will seeking Monotheistic Unity and collectivity. The imam, the spiritual leader, is the manifestation of collectivity. He is a symbol of the society of Monotheistic Unity, a society without discrimination or distinctions. He is the implementor of the Islamic system, who is bound to Monotheistic Unity and is commanded only by God (Sura XXI, 73). The spiritual leader does not represent any group's special interests. He is above all the problem solver and the architect of the progressive society of Monotheistic Unity. He represents neither national nor tribal interest. He has no ties at all. The moment he establishes ties, his Spiritual Leadership is immediately drained and he becomes, as a government, the tool of the dominating classes of the world, riding the backs of others.

Those in the government are not the spiritual leaders of Monotheistic Unity, they are the leaders of dualism and tyranny. The contrast between the Spiritual Leadership of 'Ali and the government of Mo'aviyeh and the manner in which the Spiritual Leadership of 'Ali was alienated in the government of Mo'aviyeh simultaneously illustrate the fundamental difference between Spiritual Leadership and government as well as how Spiritual Leadership become alienated from itself.[42],[43] From the very beginning, 'Ali refused the offer by those in

power of the leadership of the government and the representa-
tion of power. He rejected the invitation of Ebn Abbas and
Abu Sofyan.[44] Had he listened to these two, he would have
gone against the principle of Spiritual Leadership and would
no longer have been a representative of Monotheistic Unity.
These two represented two tribes. They told 'Ali that, as the
chiefs of two large branches of the Qoreysh, they would swear
allegiance to him. They were the chiefs of two groups of the
Qoreysh — two groups which ruled the world dualistically in the
name of Islam for seven hundred years, two groups which
became the sole ruling powers on earth — who both said, "Let
us swear allegiance to you. As soon as we do so, no one would
dare to oppose you." And they were right. Had 'Ali joined
them, his leadership would have been solidified. But then 'Ali
would no longer have been 'Ali, he would have been the
representative of the power and the coalition of these two branches of the Qoreysh. With his very "no", 'Ali declared his
Spiritual Leadership. With this very "no", he became an im-
mortal spiritual leader.

It was with this very "no" that two ideologies — one which in-
tended to transform Islam into an instrument of power and a
means of domination (the establishment of a government) and
another which wanted human beings to become leaders in the
Islamic system — were separated from one another. This very "no"
was contrary to all religions and ideologies in which the forces of
spiritual Mission, those supporting the continual spiritual Mission,
as well as the supporters of the ideological government have been
and are being absorbed. 'Ali's Islam remained and 'Ali's Spritual
Leadership became a model for everyone including all the
dynamic forces in the Islamic society.

Had 'Ali not said "no," he would not have become the
representative of God and the implementor of the Qur'an; he
would have been a representative of reactionism, of tribal,
familial, and class powers, powers which Islam had come to
abolish from human society. That is why 'Ali did not accept.
"Greetings to 'Ali," for he was a great man. How untrue it is
when it is said that, because 'Ali was busy with the Prophet's
burial arrangements, he did not pay attention to what was to
become a leadership. The Prophet's life and death were
devoted to Monotheistic Unity and God, to human freedom
and Islam. It would have been impossible to tell 'Ali, "Human
freedom is being ignored; Spiritual Leadership is left unat-

tended; hurry," And for him to answer, "Wait until I bury the Prophet and then I will come." This is impossible. This is the negation of Monotheistic Unity. The issue at hand was not that of the Islamic Spiritual Leadership. It concerned the coalition between the chiefs. How could 'Ali be involved in such games? In any case, these two wanted to join with 'Ali as the representatives of two powers. 'Ali refused to accept, saying, "This is not Spiritual Leadership; I am the proof of the principle of Spiritual Leadership, not an agent of a class, a race, or a tribe." The second characteristic of our precepts in evaluation is this: If we see a ruler who is dependent on a class, that is, who is serving class dictatorship, and at the same time claiming that his government is an Islamic one, it is a trick. We have precepts, we have 'Ali, and we have 'Ali's government.

In accordance with the general principle of Spiritual Leadership, we all have spiritual missions in an Islamic system. We must exercise and move towards becoming spiritual leaders, free ourselves from the webs of physical and mental relationships with dualism, free ourselves from autocracy and the desire to be master over someone else or be someone else's instrument, and free ourselves from dependencies in order to be deserving of the leadership of the infallible imam, in order to make possible the return to the natural self and the return to the government of Spiritual Leadership. Hence, appropriate to this principle is a society of Spiritual Leadership. By removing the obstacles and implementing this principle—to make it widespread—the establishment of an Islamic government will be possible.

The characteristics of the spiritual leader, the imam, have been enumerated in several Qur'anic verses. Since later on, in a discussion on Islamic government, I will deal with this subject, here, I will not elaborate further on Spiritual Leadership.

Thus far I have discussed Monotheistic Unity, Spiritual Mission, and the Point of Return. We have discussed Justice, and we have seen that it is a path on which progress will become possible. We have seen that, in Spiritual Leadership, the imam is the agent of Monotheistic Unity, not the representative of autocracy, not the representative of a class society—we know that every system has an imam, a spiritual leader. A heathenistic nation has an imam, too, as does every system. For example, Gaullism in France certainly has an imam; Willy Brandt is the imam of the German system. Both heathenism and Monotheistic Unity have imams. In heathenism, however, the imam represents the group which has monopolized power.

The third characteristic of an imam is that he is not an autocrat;[45] the imam is not a representative of any group. He must free himself from any sort of dependency, but in action, he is obligated to carry out Islam and Monotheistic Unity, and he must lead the society toward Monotheistic Unity within the framework of the Islmaic system and on the path of Justice (Sura VI, 15). He cannot play favorites with anyone and he cannot choose anyone he wishes to rule and take advantage of the people. Beyond the regulations of the Islamic system, he has neither the power nor the right to interfere, to pursuade or dissuade. Now, when we look at the Prophet's treatment of the murderer of Hamzah, we see that it follows this principle. This man was the murderer of the Prophet's own uncle, but as soon as he was converted to Islam, the Prophet could not renounce him saying, 'Since you are the murderer of my uncle, I refuse to accept your conversion to Islam and I will have you beheaded," No, he was the murderer of the Prophet's uncle during the Age of Ignorance *(jaheliyyat)*, before Islam; but, since the Prophet was a spiritual leader, he could not say that the man, having killed his uncle, would not be accepted as a Moslem, because during the Age of Ignorance, people had committed other mistakes, too.

Islam is a path, a path to freedom, and it cannot be closed to anyone; it must be open to all. Your duty is to free that fierce murderer in order to transform him into a complete, elevated human being. This is the duty of Spiritual Leadership. By acting in this way, you and he will attain a united identity. And this is actually what happened. The murderer who had torn out and eaten the heart of the Prophet's uncle found a common identity with the Prophet in Islam.

Let us compare our own behavior with that of the Prophet in order to realize how misguided we might be: We join in alliance and break with people every day. Is it for the sake of Islam? No, it is for the sake of "I" who consider myself to be "infallibly perfect." In appearance we are Moslems, but we are actually the proponents of dualism. When we join in alliance with someone, he becomes for us the embodiment of perfections, when our exalted self has been offended and we break with him, we drag him through muck. This kind of behavior is that of a leader of dualism, not the spiritual leader of Monotheistic Unity. Let us awaken, free ourselves, become the spiritual leaders of Monotheistic Unity, take the hands of the men and women sunk in the muck of dualism, pull them out, and cleanse them under the rays of the sun of Monotheistic Unity.

To summarize briefly, these five principles are the fundamental principles which make up the system of evaluation and guidance. Islam and the Qur'an correspond completely with these fundamental principles, and it could be no other way. Therefore, every time that we want to know the views of Islam concerning an issue — an actual, continual issue — our scientific system should comprise these five principles. With this system, we have studied marriage (see a series of articles called "The Islamic Family" *("Khanevadeh-ye Eslami)* in *Maktab-e Mobarez)*. If you, yourself, want to solve a problem, you can investigate it using this system. You will see how extensive the horizon of vision is, and how clear the problem becomes.

We will study Islamic government using this method and within this system: Islamic government is the actualization and the realization of these five principles in the society. Islamic government itself reflects these five fundamental principles. We want to make up a government (the principle of Spiritual Leadership) which translates the demands of Monotheistic Unity into an Islamic system (principles 1 and 2) and puts it on the direct path of continual activism and relativism (the principle of Justice), leading human society towards the Point of Return, where Monotheistic Unity is manifested, where man loses completely his relationship with the Age of Ignorance, the principles of autocracy, polytheism, and separation (the principle of the Point of Return). In order for an Islamic government to be able to play such a role, it cannot be dependent on any one class. It must be a manifestation and an implementor of Islam. Hence, in accordance with these five principles and the basic principle of Monotheistic Unity, in order to bring about an Islamic government and block reactionism, we must not flock around elements of domination. Insead, we must follow a collective of elements on which this Islamic government can be established and which will prevent us from returning to a dualistic government, setting us on a direct path of Justice, towards the Point of Return and Monotheistic Unity.

For this purpose, we will follow the way of the Qur'an: First, we will deal with the negatives, that is, we will deal with the issues which must be eliminated, in order to arrive at those which must remain. First, *la* (no) and then *ella* (but/except).

NOTES

1. Ali Shari'ati, (1933-77): Iranian sociologist and lecturer on Islam who was active in the anti-Pahlavi movement.

2. See note 1 of the Preface.

3. See note 6 in Chapter 1.

4. *Natural phenomena and actual events are also guided in their genesis and motion by these five fundamental Islamic principles.*

5. N.B.: This does not refer to the events of 1978-79, as the speech was given and published in 1974.

6. Rostam: an Iranian Hercules prototype of Ferdowsi's tenth or eleventh century epic poem, the *Shahnameh* (Book of Kings).

7. Reza Khan: Reza Shah (ruled 1921-41), the founder of the Pahlavi dynasty and father of the late, deposed shah, Mohammad Reza Pahlavi.

8. Lat and 'Ozza: two of the principal idols of pre-Islamic Arabia.

9. References to the kaa'ba in pre-Islamic times.

10. One of Shah Mohammad Reza Pahlavi's generals.

11. *In passing, I would like to call to your attention a danger: We must not consider those that we are fond of as infallibly perfect. Good and beloved people must be loved, but must not be made out to be infallibly perfect beings. Then again, I must warn you that avoidance of considering anything as infallibly perfect does not mean that whenever someone speaks the truth you should say, "Since we should not accept anything as infallibly perfect, we must not accept the words of this speaker either." No, the truth must be verified logically, cleared of all ambiguities. I will speak of this later, in the section on Spiritual Leadership, and you will see that, according to the Qur'an, an imam, a spiritual leader, is one whose understanding of the word of God has reached absolute certainty. This is one of the characteristics of an imam.*

12. *How fitting are the words* al-'elm-o howal hejabol akbar- *(science is the greatest veil). Do we not witness what science in the service of domination has brought mankind, and how science has been held up as a bludgeon, actually blurring the scientific vision of mankind?*

13. *The U.S. and the U.S.S.R. spend 83 percent of the world's research funds. Of the remaining 17 percent, Western Europe and Japan spend 13 percent and the remaining 4 percent is spent by the rest of the world. In other words, the active mental forces are concentrated in the West, and the rest of the world consumes their products. And within what framework do they produce? Within the framework of their own domination over the world!*

14. *I was talking to a Jew and I said, "You claim that you are the chosen people; the fact that you consider yourselves superior to others is opposed to the principle of Monotheistic Unity." He said, "It is merely an expression of truth; the rest does not matter; thus, we do our duty as the chosen people and try to guide mankind in any way we can." I asked, "In any way you can? He replied, "Was Marx not a Jew?" I said, "Yes." He asked, "Trotsky?" I answered, "He, too." He asked, "Max Weber?" I said, "Yes, but they did not believe in God, neither did they accept religion." He said, "That does not matter; their duty was to guide, and they did it." We, too, do our duty.*

15. *I had planned to mention this in the section   on the Cult of Personality, as I will also do; however, this particular part does not concern the Cult of Personality.*

16. Jamshid: mythological Iranian king who is supposed to have founded the Persian kingdom.

17. *Now, ignoring the fact that it has separated religion from politics and extended its own power, the regime then says, "The spiritual world and religion must also become part of the system."*

18. Abuzar: one of the Prophet Mohammad's companions.

19. Mohammad Mosaddeq, (1880-1967): Iranian Prime Minister (1951-53), influential in the nationalization of the Iranian oil industry, who almost succeeded in deposing the shah in 1953. Tudehs: Iranian Communist party, founded in the early 1940s and banned by the former shah.

20. Pishehvari: a leader of the Communist Tudeh Party of Iran at the time.

21. *The same situation exists in Iran. Remember Eqbal and Alam quarrelling.*[22] *One said: You have not comprehended his majesty's intentions. The other said: No, you have not; I have.*

22. Eqbal and Alam: influential political leaders, both having held the office of Prime Minister at different times, during the reign of Mohammad Reza Pahlavi.

23. Othman (d. 656): third Caliph of Moslems. Mo'aviyeh: founder of the first Moslem dynasty (see note 6 in Chapter 1). Mansur (d. 775): second Abbassid Caliph, regarded as the real founder of the Abbassid Caliphate (see note 6 in Chapter 1).

24. 'Ali ebn Abitaleb: see note 5 in Chapter 1. Saqifeh: meeting place where the important tribal leaders gathered after the death of Mohammad to decide on his successor.

25. Hoseyniyeh Ershad: a religious center in Tehran, established in 1965, which attracted great crowds to its lectures on Islam.

26. *The problem has gotten so far out of hand that today dozens of books and articles have been published on the subject by revolutionary elements in the West. Alas, the "leftists" in the dominated countries are not only behind in this respect, but they even advocate the "opiate of sex."*

27. *How interesting the reading of the Shahnameh* (Book of Kings) *is, wherein Keykhorsrow is described in his solitude as searching to escape the fate of Jamshid and finally giving up power.*[28]

28. Keykhosrow: one of the mythological kings of Ferdowsi's Shahnameh. Shahnameh and Jamshid: See not 6, in Chapter 1.

29. References to bas-reliefs and engravings such as those of the Sassanians (226-641 AD.) found at the Achaemenian (539-330 B.C.) tomb sites at Naqsh-e Rostam in Iran.

30. Reference to claims made by the late shah, Mohammad Reza Pahlavi, on numerous occasions that he had seen in his

dreams various holy figures who had given him certain directives. Several of these dreams are recorded in his book *Mission
for My Country.*

31. *Since he recognizes power as the basis of all things and
    himself a symbol of it, even unconsciously, in the
    blasphemous lie he tells as his dream, he states that it is not he
    who goes to the imam, but the imam who seeks "audience"
    with him!*

32. *If this amalgamation is influenced through the interference
    of outside elements, it will deviate from the direction of
    Monotheistic Unity and a united identity, and it will be
    dispersed.*

33. Safavids (1501-1736): Iranian dynasty which established
    Shi'ite Islam as the state religion. Shah Esma'il: founder of
    the dynasty. Shah Soltan Hoseyn: last of the Safavids, over-
    thrown by Afghan invaders.

34. *Laborer, here, has a deeper meaning. A laborer is not merely
    one who works, it is one who both works and is mistreated. It
    is he who is the slave to a system of which the political,
    economic social, and cultural organizations suck the last vital
    drop out of him.*

35. *That is why it is said, "Paradise is under the feet of mothers."
    Today, Western societies have devalued the rearing of human
    beings. They depict motherhood as demeaning. In Islam,
    nothing equals the production of human beings, that is,
    training relative, active humans, humans who are spiritual
    leaders seeking Monotheistic Unity.*

36. Abu Moslem: an Iranian of obscure origin who led a revolt
    against the Umayyads (see note 6 in Chapter 1) in 747 AD,
    which ultimately ended in the overthrow of the dynasty in 750
    AD.

37. *There are certain concepts which the enemies of freedom
    have misrepresented merely to dupe the people. These
    enemies have made these false concepts commonplace in the
    minds of the people through constant repetition. The issue
    must be clarified by repeating the correct concept; therefore,
    although I have explained this issue elsewhere, I find it ap-
    propriate to repeat it here.*

38. *From the Tradition (Hadith) of the Prophet: Neither is Arab superior to non-Arab nor non-Arab superior to Arab. Neither is black superior to white nor white to black. Superiority belongs only to the pious.*

39. See note 2 in the Preface.

40. *Maktab-e Mobarez, XIII.*

41. Banisadr's interpretation of the verse, as his Persian translation indicates, differs from standard interpretations, an example of which is, "But man wishes to do wrong (even) in the time in front of him" (See 70-71 of this text for the verse in context.)

42. *How mistaken was Ebn Khaldun when he considered Mo'aviyeh the rightful representative of the general spirit of the Islmaic establishment. Is it not surprising that a person such as he could take such a wrong turn in spite of the obviousness of the Spiritual Leadership of 'Ali? The Spiritual Leadership of 'Ali, the reason for the Spiritual Leadership, is inherently natural and acceptable.*

    In looking at the government of Mo'aviyeh, we must look at the alienation of Spiritual Leadership from itself and recognize the factors of the transformation of Spiritual Leadership into government. Ebn Khaldun considers government as the essential principle. The importance of the contrast between the Spiritual Leadership of 'Ali and the government of Mo'aviyeh should show clearly to the man who has lost his way that Spiritual Leadership is not mere fantasy, but it can materialize. It must show him that even government—the Spiritual Leadership of 'Ali replaced the government of Othman—can be retransformed to Spiritual Leadership, thereby changing the instruments of domination into inherent leadership.

43. See notes 5 ('Ali) and 6 (Mo'aviyeh) of Chapter 1 *(Othman)* Ebn Khaldun (mentioned in Banisadr's footnote): Fourteenth century Arab historian and sociologist.

44. Ebn Abbas: founder of the Abbasid dynasty (750-1258); see note 6 in Chapter 1. Abu Sofyan: the father of Mo'aviyeh (see note 6 in Chapter 1).

45. *See Ayatollah Khomeini's* Islamic Government.

3

The Characteristics Held Negative
by an Islamic Government

In order to find out what must not be and what must be, we must have a division in time—what must not be at what time. Since an Islamic government will not be exactly the same in the beginning as it will be in its following periods, what are those things that must not exist in the beginning, in an Islamic government, in order for it to be able to retain its position of moving toward its destination of Monotheistic Unity? We must distinguish between short and long periods of time, and we must clarify what elements must not exist in these two kinds of periods. On the basis of these five principles, I will enumerate the "no's," the characteristics held negative by an Islamic government:

Not a Nation Based on a
Dominance Relationship

This means searching out the origins of dualism in society, in politics, in the economy, and in other areas; that is, we should find out how classes and groups have come to exist and how they are classified in the society, and also gain an understanding of the methods of economic amassment—today's world economy consists of various economies which serve amassed powers. The workings of amassed economic powers must be methodically studied and destroyed at the root.

If we want to draw a picture of an Islamic government for

Iran, since that is our country and it provides a background for our thoughts, we must study the centers and the operational mechanisms of the amassment of power in Iran. We must also understand what sort of relationship these centers of amassed power have with centers of amassed power throughout the world.

Not Based on Positive Neutrality and a Dominance Relationship on a Worldwide Scale

From here on, we must study the general system of the world as a system of domination and study its economic and political (as well as cultural and social) relationships throughout the world—the relationship between dominator and dominated.

These are elements which are negative and must be eliminated. An Islamic government must abolish these negatives in the ultimate society based on the first principle (Monotheistic Unity), the second principle (Spiritual Mission), the third principle (Spiritual Leadership), the path of movement (Justice), and the direction of the movement (the Point of Return). In other words, if we establish a government, as Modarres says, that government must follow the principle of negative equilibrium (the first principle, Monotheistic Unity) in order for the society to be set into motion (the principle of Spiritual Mission), and in this movement it will become a pioneer and model for the world (the principle of Spiritual Leadership). This movement toward an ultimate society must travel on the path of Justice, that is, the path of relativism and activism (the principle of Justice), if we are to be a model system for the rest of the world, a system which human beings have been trying throughout the course of history but as yet been unable to attain (the principle of the Point of Return). Negative equilibrium means obstructing the path to domination. Not only must the domination in existence be eliminated, but the path to any recreation of this sort of realtionship must be obstructed. You can, therefore, see that it is possible to have a very clear theoretical base. The most fundamental of problems can be solved within the theoretical system based on common laws.

As Moslems, we cannot agree with any type of domination, whether it be political, economic, cultural, or social. Therefore, the design of an Islamic government must reflect these five principles in all its aspects. It must understand these dominations and try to negate them. The organization and structure of an Islamic government must be able to seize the amassed power of these dominator agents and abolish domination altogether. The instruments of the amassment of power — the amassment of political, economic, social, and intellectual power (powers have instruments through which they concentrate in certain areas such as the military, the economy, and capital, creating false needs and demands in order to create a market, and so on) — must be completely eliminated in a society under an Islamic government, since these instruments make such amassment possible. Consequently, not only must we study these powers, but we must also negate them. They are the "no's" of an Islamic government.

Not Beliefs or Ideologies
as Instruments of Power

We must note that an Islamic government is a government of ideology, not a government governing ideology. This is the same "no", the same actual continual issue, which has always existed throughout history: groups in the name of an idea have attained power, but later have made the original idea an instrument of power, thus metamorphosing it. In an Islamic government, the limitations on the actions of the spiritual leader, the imam, are defined on the basis of the fundamental principles and guidelines of the Islamic system. That is, an Islamic government will carry out an ideology, it will depend on an ideology, but it will not dominate ideas.

Even now, ideologies are metamorphosed by new powers and become instruments. This is common throughout the world. In all the countries of the world, ideology is one of the major instruments in the service of power. Therefore, it is not peculiar to religion. Any ideology which become official, which becomes an instrument of power, becomes the opiate of the masses, because power, while using "ideology" in order to legitimize itself, also becomes a bludgeon. Let someone even think of making a move against the power and the power will tag it, for example, anti-Marxist, anti-Islamic, and damnable.

The bludgeon of "heretic" is always in the hands of the dominating power, which will break the bones of anyone who would dare make the slightest move to oppose it (Sura XL, 26).

Lin Piao, who up to the other day was in charge of everything in China, who was proclaimed by the Congress the successor to Mao, the man who had even written the Introduction to the Red Book (the holy book), suddenly disappeared. Later, it was proclaimed that he had been killed because Mao had told someone that he had who-knows-what intentions. What is the explanation? As one of Mao's most trusted associates, who had also been approved by the Congress, he had been chosen as a precautionary scapegoat. They claimed that he had become a revisionist and most likely hoped to plan a coup d'etat. In any case, he had given up the "religion."

Therefore, it is not religion alone which is the opiate of the masses. Any religion or ideology which is put at the service of power, and does not control power, becomes the opiate of the masses. It makes no difference what school it belongs to. Do you think that if you make Islam the instrument of a system it will not become an opiate? Because Islam is a religion based upon common laws and nature to free mankind of the entanglement of continual actual issues, it cannot become an opiate of the masses unless it is mutilated, as it has been by the present regime, which has made it official.

Therefore, in an Islamic government, ideology must not become the instrument of government, but government must become the instrument of ideology. In practice, government must be the expression of the Islamic ideology; that is, the distinction between theory and pratice must be eliminated, which requires certain safeguards to assure that ideology will govern. In order to prevent there ever being a gap between ideology and the behavior of the government, any time that we see that our government is about to take some step, right then and there we must see whether or not this action will correspond with the ideology. If we see that there is a discrepancy, safeguards must be devised to prevent the possibility of such an occurrence. The discrepancy must be corrected immediately, otherwise, it will become larger and larger later on, until a caliphate like that of the Umayyads or Abbassids and the monarchy is once again formed.

Not Based on the Cult of Personality

In order to create safeguards in an Islamic society, under an Islamic government, we must fight against the Cult of Personality. No one should become a "bludgeon."

Certain safeguards must be established to prevent the monopolization of power and decision making by one government and its symbol, a chief or a shah, and to prevent the society from becoming an instrument of governmental decisions. An Islamic government should not consist of those who are sitting in high places and making decisions without the supervision or participation of the people, who serve only to implement these orders. Such is contrary to all the five fundamental principles, because then the people become instruments rather than human beings.

Not Based on "The End Justifies the Means"

Another safeguard is that an Islamic government does not have the right to follow the philosophy that "the end justifies the means," which is a philosophy of absolute power and autocracy. According to this philosophy, the commission of any crime is not only allowed but even necessary in reaching a goal.

This is the view of Machiavelli. Before Machiavelli, similar views were expressed in *One Thousand and One Nights* by those in power. It has always existed everywhere and still does. In Asian, European, American (Watergate is still being talked about), and African soceieties, this has always been and still is the slogan. In Iran, for example, they talk about the "requisites of monarchy," meaning that "his majesty" is concerned, but, well, it cannot be helped; the good of the monarchy requires that the youth of the country be shot (although he has compassion for them!). When the goal is power, homicide is justified.

But this philosophy is not that of an Islamic government, in which the means must correspond absolutely with the end. This is precisely what religious precepts are all about. The precepts must correspond with the principles. The precepts of an Islamic government—that is, the means that an Islamic government employs in order to achieve its goal—must correspond directly with its goal. For instance, if someone says that

63

his purpose is to attain a government based on Monotheistic Unity, but at the same time he imports a number of automobiles and distributes them only to his friends and followers under the pretext that they are to be used to check on various districts to see whether or not the class structure has been eliminated, we must tell him, "No, we do not accept what you are doing, because you are actually establishing classes; you are not following the path of Monotheistic Unity, you are walking along a path which will end in a dualistic class society." Russia, Cuba, and others have followed this path and have come to this same dead end.

Not Based on
Prohibiting Evaluation and Criticism

The soceity must make use of everything at its disposal in the way of evaluation and criticism. Through the revitalization and spread of the precepts of "encouraging good" and "discouraging evil," an evaluative and critical society must be established (Sura IX, 71). This is the goal of an Islamic government. Therefore, an Islamic government is not one afraid of criticism. On the contrary, it must welcome criticism. It must welcome a call for good deeds and provide the possibilities for their implementation. The pretext that criticism and evaluation would weaken the government (which is precisely what we hear nowadays — they tell us not to breathe, it is against the White Revolution!) — is not representative of an Islamic government.

An Islamic government proposes to create an evaluative and critical society. The obligation in Islam to encourage good and discourage evil, based on the five fundamental principles, safeguards the participation of the people in the management of their own affairs. Self-criticism — which is popular nowadays (but not practiced) — which Islam has called the great spiritual struggle, must be valued. And in order to form a monotheistically unified human being, the fundamental principles of education in an Islamic society must be Islamic principles.

Not Based on Government as an
Instrument of Domination

An Islamic government must free society by abolishing

government as an instrument of domination or as a dominating power in the society; this must be the direction of movement. But we cannot expect that from the very first day that the government is abolished it will be automatically transformed into Spiritual Leadership. For centuries our brains have been filled with the idea that we cannot survive without a government. It is possible to return government to its own nature, which is Spiritual Leadership, as is indicated by the Spiritual Leadership of 'Ali and the management in revolutionary times of countries which, in our own time, have lived through long years of revolution.

A most important aspect of the great spiritual struggle is that we can free ourselves of the kind of thoughts which have been imprinted on our minds as absolute. The government must be transformed to be set in the direction of a return to natural Spiritual Leadership, since, on the basis of the five principles, everyone must participate in the management of public affairs. If everyone does so, the management of public affairs will require no boss or anyone who would take power into his own hands. When power is in the hands of an individual, it becomes amassed, that is, it absorbs the rest of the active forces of the society, destroys them and the course of their growth, and prevents the soceity from moving toward Monotheistic Unity.

NOTES

1. *Because the strongest foundation of dualism lies in our thoughts, if dualistic thinking—which results in thinking in terms of classes, supposing oneself superior, the center of the universe, and seeking autocracy—is not eliminated, human beings will reamin in their present state and no serious change will occur. The foundations of dualistic thinking must be destroyed in order for human beings to become free. That is why it has been said that challenging the self is the great spiritual struggle.*

4

The Characteristics Held Positive
by an Islamic Government

We have discussed the characteristics which are regarded as negative in order to safeguard the Islamic government. Now, let us see what solution Islam suggests for the implementation of these safeguards.

Negative Equilibrium

An Islamic society will follow the principle of negative equilibrium in its relations with the rest of the world. An Islamic society is a society of spiritual leaders; therefore, it cannot dominate other societies. That is, the government must not be allowed to dominate other units or socieities, nor to become dominated by them. 'Ali was the first in history who believed in this principle and acted accordingly in his dealings with Moslem nations. 'Ali, as the expresser and the implementor of the five principles, as well as of negative equilibrium, was always opposed to allowing the Arab elements to dominate the non-Arabs and rightly believed that domination would corrupt both the dominator and the dominated. For this reason, the Pan-Arabists, and those who believed in the necessity of the world domination of the Arabs, gathered around Mo'aviyeh and founded the Arab Empire. And now it has been several centuries since the dominating Arabs and dominated non-Arabs have been ruined by Western domination.

We cannot say that because we are Moslems, we must dominate others on the grounds that they are heathen nations, saying, in effect, "To hell with them, we will beat them over the heads and rob them." Such is the behavior of a group of thieves who divide their spoils equally among themselves. The end of such an Islamic government would be the same as that of a group of thieves; that is, after a while, they would begin to quarrel amongst themselves, which is invariably the norm. When you take someone else's belongings away from him to amass wealth, he becomes thin and you become fat. And once again you return to square one.

Therefore, in our attitude towards the world, we do not propose to dominate others nor to be dominated by others. In this case, our military duty is simply defensive. That is, our military role in the world must be defensive, and we will never mobilize an army; we will never have an army for the purpose of dominating others. That is, we will never engage in an aggressive war. Why not? Because holy struggle (*jahad*) is one of our religious precepts, corresponding totally with the fundamental principles. This crusade serves the purpose of eliminating dualism and creating Monotheistic Unity. We know that in domination there is no Monotheistic Unity, but there is dualism: one dominates and another is dominated — no Monotheistic Unity at all. We must liberate; in other words, we must return others to their nature. This is the meaning of holy struggle, doing our duty for Spiritual Leadership, removing obstacles, freeing captives, and facilitating their participation in the Spiritual Mission, in other words, spreading the principle of Spiritual Mission; we can then demonstrate our nonconformity with domination, and then we will be spiritual strugglers. This is exactly what Modarres meant when he correctly said that the basis of our religion is passive neutrality. We cannot be a society of dominators; therefore, on neither an international scale nor a regional scale will we seek to prepare ourselves militarily to dominate others.

Thus, our course will be one of independence, independence in the sense which we have spoken of, the course of negative equilibrium. By doing this, we will help to free and reactivate all the existing innate abilities in the world. Our holy struggle is to make a model of ourselves to set before the rest of the world (Sura XXII, 78).[1]

Following negative equilibrium, we will remove ourselves from the system of world domination, and, by freeing ourselves, we will be able to become a model for the entire world, hence, performing our duty of Spiritual Leadership.

Leaving the System of World Domination and Destroying Centers of Amassed Power

It is our duty to completely eliminate the centers of amassed power within our society that are connected to centers of amassed power throughout the world, and to prevent Islamic society from being absorbed in the worldwide system of domination. Not becoming absorbed is multifaceted. In other words, we must free ourselves of the slavery of the value system controlling consumption, the system which dominates production, the value system which dominates political activity, in short, the value system which dominates the cultural activities of the world today.

In our type of consumption and production and in our political relations with the rest of the world, we must follow negative equilibrium. Based on this course of action, the economic programs must be those which will bring to fruition natural human abilities. We will prepare programs for the society that will give people the opportunity to use their minds and bodies and reap the benefits equally as brothers. The fundamental course we will follow is to sever relations with the dominating systems. That is, we must break those relationships which have now been created, whether in the area of economic production, economic consumption, the military, or whatever, in order to obstruct the amassment of power at the top, which results in autocracy and tyranny at the top and absolute instability, insecurity, and living in dualism.

The Transformation of Power from the Top to the Base

We have said that the government as a god, a demonic power, a pharaoh, etc., must be eliminated. In order to do this, we must return power from the top to the base, the masses, to whom the power originally belonged. So long as there are power centers, power cannot be distributed throughout society. Therefore, the program, the movement, and an Islamic government must be directed towards a gradual redistribution of power throughout society in order to ensure the creation of a society of Monotheistic Unity and eliminate the possibility of the regression of the government to dualism. And, also, this government must overcome its self-alienation and hold only a leadership role consisting of the management of the society to move towards Monotheistic Unity.

When we want to change the direction, that is, when we want to reverse the concentration of power from the top to the bottom, we want the existing power centers to be eliminated and power to be gradually distributed reasonably throughout the society on the basis of the principle of Monotheistic Unity. The society will then find a common identity: It will become a congregation which is the manifestation of Monotheistic Unity. In order for this to come about, Islam must govern the Islamic society. In other words, human relationships within the boundaries of our society must be rechannelled along the Islamic path. Within this society, man can become free, and the abilities of all the members of the society will be used. It is only thus that you will see the great difference between the results of limited thought in closed centers and that which thirty million human beings can bring about (for example, in Iran today).[2] This cannot be accomplished except by:

The Universalization and Revitalization of Holy Struggle

What is holy struggle [*jahad*]? It is the struggle to attain Monotheistic Unity and God. In order to undertake this great mission, we must train ourselves as Islamic soldiers. We must look to see what means the enemy has at its disposal and equip ourselves with better ones. Otherwise, if we only have what the enemy has, there is a chance of defeat.

Holy struggle is based on the fundamental principles and, like those principles, it is constant and universal. That is, we must be in a constant holy struggle. Of course, holy struggle requires weapons *(Sura VIII, 60)*. You cannot struggle without weapons. The most significant and the sharpest weapon is creativity. In holy struggle, imitation signifies defeat. An army of strugglers which imitates, like those which dissolve into larger ones, has all the force of a puff of smoke. We must seek out and use the best methods for victory. As you know, it has been said that those who are to participate in the ultimate revolution are continually armed and have freed themselves of all dependencies and desires in order to identify themselves with their common goal (Sura IX, 24). (Our revolutions are only preparations for the ultimate revolution: Continual Spiritual Mission. By continuing to sleep, we cannot attain the Revolution of the Twelfth Imam.[3] It can be achieved only through Continual Spiritual Mission.) They have freed themselves of all dependency and are pioneers of the revolution of Monotheistic Unity.

We must not think that our expectation of revolution is merely hoping for revolution. Our expectation is not mere expectation, it is a movement towards that destination. We are moving. The earth will never be without a representative of God. Our Continual Spiritual Mission, our constant movement, will provide the opportunity for his presence. We must be in a state of uprising at all times. We must be in a state of constant holy struggle. Holy struggle cannot have a day of rest. We must not think that, although holy struggle was a religious mandate fourteen centuries ago, it is not so now. Every day, and especially today, we must struggle and become martyrs of holy struggle. Being martyred means being freed of all dependency and self-alienation, a pioneer of the spiritual Mission of Monotheistic Unity.

We will not attack foreigners, but we will participate in the struggle for freedom anywhere, in accordance with the principles of holy struggle. We will assist in any way we can other movements formed to free nations from domination. Every action to liberate others corresponds with our principles. If any people request help to expel a foreign army from their country, we will act if we can. But we will not attack others in order to free them. Our premise is that they, too, should work for it. They should liberate themselves. Of course, our holy struggle, our liberation, and our becoming a model will change the thought structure of the world. This will help in the abandonment of enslaving beliefs and the instigation of motion. In the absence of the Twelfth Imam, our holy struggle consists of self-construction, acting in accordance with Spiritual Leadership, and the defense of our freedom against aggression.

We Shi'ites believe in defense, meaning the defense of ourselves. Holy war was not required of women. But, defense is required of all, including children of all ages and all men and women. Why is it that none of us knows how to discharge this religious duty? You see how negligent our religious leaders have been! They have paid so much attention to the protocols of such things as going to the toilet, but they have absolutely forgotten to teach us the protocols of defense. Without holy struggle, the principles and precepts of Islam are set aside, as is the present case. From the day when the duty of defense was given over to a specialized group, the army, Moslems fell into misfortune and became captives of domestic and foreign mercenaries.

Defense is a general issue. If a government stifles the whole society, that society must rise up in defense of Islam and of its freedom. Defense is a multifaceted duty. It is military, proselytizing, political, etc. Thus, when an anti-Islamic government begins to propagandize against us, we should not fail to respond in kind, thinking that we are merely warriors, and that propaganda is not part of defense. We must make our presence known everywhere and reveal their lies. We must elucidate their lies and deceptions. Of course, we should guard against acting in ways that do not correspond with our goal, which would result in crimes against human dignity — our uprising primarily intends to allow human beings to regain their dignity. This task requires education and continual preparation in various areas.

Holy struggle is a form of worship and, like other forms of worship, it is an exercise of freedom. To perform it, we require education, creativity, exercise, and living in a state of constant preparedness. Holy struggle does not seek superiority (the first principle of Monotheistic Unity). It strives for Monotheistic Unity, that is, for God. But we cannot undertake holy struggle on our own behalf. Holy struggle must be fought for ideology. And this is the meaning of "life is only for ideology and holy struggle." A holy struggle which is not based on ideology is not an Islamic holy struggle. Therefore, our touchstone to distinguish a true holy struggle is whether it corresponds with our ideology. Our touchstone is Islamic ideology. Holy struggle must intend to set the society in motion within an Islamic framework and not the contrary, as, for example, when the people make the least effort, they are told, "Don't you dare; this holy struggle of yours is not an Islamic one but a heathenistic one."[4] It is heathenistic when we ask the Viet-
72

namese, "Why are you futilely fooling around with the Americans?" Islam has said, "Do not endanger yourself; such opposes Islam."

Holy struggle must also correspond with Continual Spiritual Mission, because, if Continual Spiritual Mission is not constantly accompanied by continual uprising and preparedness, it will be meaningless. You must be constantly ready to serve, not merely ready to offer yourself whenever you are called, but you must prepare yourself to always be in the front lines, alert, without being called.

Today, in science, you see that if you neglect it for one year, you will be behind, and you will stay behind. You see that, in industrial workshops, the workers have continual training. This kind of ongoing education and exercise was our method in the beginning, but, little by little, we have abandoned it.

The blame must be laid on our learned religious scholars, who have caused the dissolution of this methodology. Although they themselves write books on the principles and precepts of religion, they are guilty of neglecting one of the most essential religious precepts. Today, when you ask one of our theological students how to use a rifle, you will find out that he has never even had a rifle in his hand.

In Islam, there is no church and there is no need for a priest in the church. Islam is supposed to train spiritual leaders and holy strugglers. But, alas, a hundred times alas. . .

NOTES

1. *The West has made a model for a dualistic society, dragging the world like sheep running after the grass of "pleasure," and sinking it every day in anxiety, etc. Who can deny that the model of a society based on Monotheistic Unity will not lead the world to ultimate revolution?*

2. *Of course, you will say that after all, this number includes children as well as adults. Do not think, however, that children cannot participate in thinking. In the least, the child creates an atmosphere in which a problem is set forth and helps those who are able to think. Thus, he shares in thinking and, as a member of the society, raises questions. For example, when the population increases, what is to be done in the area of production? If all participate in solving the problem, the answer will assuredly be closer to that which Spiritual Leadership would provide.*

3. *Revolution of the Twelfth Imam:* reference to the general Shi'ite belief that the Twelfth Imam, Mahdi, will come out of occultation to establish Justice in the world.

4. *As you know, recently in Thailand, whose guerrillas are mostly Moslems, the Iranian government has seen fit to warn the Moslem guerrillas that what they are doing is counter to Islam. A person by the name of Dr. Khorasani or Khonsari was sent there to give a speech concerning the basic opposition of Islam to such actions!*

5

Executive Safeguards of
an Islamic Government

I will only deal with these safeguards briefly and will finish my discussion on government. Let us suppose that there are certain groups which together form God's party [hezbollah] and, as God has promised, "Indeed, the people of God will be victorious," and we become victorious, what, then, should we do to avoid becoming the demonic power of the time? We must devise certain safeguards which, while hindering our becoming demonic powers, will also prevent others from taking the opportunity to become powerful, to dismiss us, and to establish the demonic system once again.

The Islamic Army and Society

The principal tool of a class society which enables the amassment of power in centers is the army. The army plays two roles in war: offensive and defensive. There are also two kinds of stratagems, two kinds of tactics, and two kinds of weapons: offensive and defensive.

In organizing the army, we will make its duty purely defensive. But, this will not prevent us from studying the offensive stratagems and tactics of others, because we must always place ourselves in such a situation that, if attacked, we can be victorious. Therefore, we must always know what the enemy is up to. This is quite different from preparing ourselves to attack, which we will not do. This idea will influence the shaping of the army. Thus, in training, for the most part, we will stop at training for strategic and tactical defense. And in military production, we will consider those elements of defense in direct relation to the strategic and tactical offense of the enemy. We must provide ourselves with defensive weapons which will counteract the offensive weapons of the enemy. This will be the basis of our efforts.

One idea which has been imprinted on our minds as an absolute truth is that the army can only exist as it does presently, and in no other form, that an army is a disciplined power, a segment taken and separated from and made dominant over the rest of society which has been disarmed. Such is an army, and so it is everywhere in the world. Of course, there are various colorful curtains of deceit hiding the truth from the people, preventing them from knowing that the army is the spinal column of the government. It is only when an event such as that in France occurs—when de Gaulle's position was extremely endangered until the army suddenly showed up in Paris and surrounded the city with tanks. Only in such situations do people realize that the primary function of such an army is to protect the governing regime.

In any case, since we are not in favor of offense, we will not have an offensive army. Our problem is to organize defense in such a way that the army would not become a means of social strangulation. On the basis of the fundamental principles and holy struggle, we must find a way in which, while we will have the best defense against foreign aggression, we will not be creating a power outside of the society which will become dominant over it, an instrument of the self-alienation of government.

As examples, I will bring up a few experiences which are related to what we are talking about. The Russian invasion of Czechoslovakia in 1968 occurred within six hours and faced no resistance. And Czechoslovakia finds itself in the situation which we are witness to, regardless of whether their claim that their proletariat government was turning into a bourgeois one and the Russians prevented it is true or false. We only want to understand why Czechoslovakia did not resist. But, how could an auxiliary army and unarmed people put up resistance? An army created by the Soviet Union for the purpose of dominating Czechoslovakia, an army whose every detail was known to the Soviets, could not even contemplate putting up a resistance. Strangely enough, under the pretext of the necessity of strengthening the army, this same experience is being repeated in Iran, and the Iranian army is being made an appendage of the American army.

And then there is the experience of Vietnam. Did the National Liberation Front have an army? It was the people who were fighting. Later, of course, they formed a regular army, but if all the people had not volunteered in this war of independence, that army would have been destroyed ten times over.

The nucleus of the Algerian Revolution consisted of only twenty-two members. The first revolutionary army which began to fight consisted of only five hundred freedom fighters. But the casualties of the National Liberation Army in the service of the Algerian Revolution came to one million people.

But, in our Islamic society, if we universalize the principle of holy struggle, since everyone must participate in this Spiritual Mission, everyone will be a spiritual leader and all will be freedom fighters. Under present conditions, we must mobilize the entire society to defend itself. Then, a foreign power will be unable to overtake us in six hours, or be able to expel us from the scene as a unit separate from society, or humiliate us, like 100 million Arabs were by some 2 million Zionists in the Arab-Israeli Six-Day War, a humiliation which still persists. Obviously, such dependent armies are very costly.

We witnessed the Iranian army in September of 1941. What bitter fruit it brought forth; it could not resist for even two hours.[1] We witnessed the Arab armies during the Six-Day War. But the Algerian army is qauite a different model, as is that of Vietnam. Hence, in conformity with the principle of Monotheistic Unity, the army must exist on all social levels and the society itself must organize its defense so that the army, as the most essential tool of a class society, of class domination, and of the amassment of power in centers, is eliminated.

In an Islamic government, the barracks are the people's house. No place, no barracks, is better than the gathering places of the people. Defense must be organized in every city and in every unit. And military training, like other training, must be given to everyone.[2]

Naturally, as far as strategic awareness and military production are concerned, an Islamic government would take care to keep the society in such a position that it would never end up

77

being caught off guard and would be able to employ all its defenses if attacked. The creature called the army, which for centuries has been dominating the wretched people under the pretext of protecting the borders, must be replaced by an army of the people. When this materializes, the most significant basis of terror for the future will have collapsed. The element which always causes self-alienation of the leadership will have been eliminated, and the society will have begun its transformation to the ultimate society of Monotheistic Unity. When I say this is the goal, you must not imagine that the army should be abolished from day one. An Islamic government must move towards this direction and base its programs concerning the army on the following: universalizing the principle of holy struggle, dissolving the army, and involving the society in its own defense and the regulation of it.

Establishing Public Supervision over the Leadership of Society

Now, we have defined our foreign relations militarily and politically. Since we will not have an offensive strategy, we will not have a political strategy; that is, we will not be a dominant political power to wheel and deal with others; we will not wheel and deal with any power in the world. We will be absolutely free of power politics. To this end, to control and supervise the political leadership of the Islamic government, the Islamic society must prepare the people to participate in the government, because if the people fail to participate, it will not be an Islamic government, that is, it will not have accepted the principle of public supervision over its actions. Mosques must become centers in which the government of God will materialize, because a mosque is a place where no one has the right to give orders to anyone. It is only God Who governs. All others are equal. It is a place where open criticism and re-evaluation must be exercised. That is, at least once a week, every unit should supervise its affairs and subject the entire society and the central leadership to criticism and re-evaluation, and revitalize and strengthen the basic principles of re-evaluation and criticism. This is a political safeguard to prevent the government from going off its course.

Then, every part of this government will follow the five fundamental principles. We do not need to specify here, for example, how "consultation" will take place, or how such-and-such an issue will be handled; therefore, I will not deal with such details, I will only briefly address the issue of "consultation" and similar questions which have been raised and which must be answered. You, yourselves, have thought about these problems, and later on you will once again hold these issues up to measure against the fundamental principles to seek practical solutions. But, these safeguards alone are not enough. Other safeguards are also required.

Economic Safeguards

Economic safeguards are necessary, since the root of the problem is that power determines who will eat more and who will eat less.

We have dealt with the principles before and we have also seen, through Qur'anic verse, what the guiding principles should be. In economic planning, all the factors must be viewed in terms of those five principles, that is, production must benefit all. Therefore, the production of items to be consumed by a special group which wishes to distinguish itself from others is unnecessary.

An Islamic government does not represent those who wish to distinguish themselves from others, it represents the collective. In the economy, production and consumption are to be based on the need of the collective. Our plans would be based on monotheistically unified movement and finding a common identity should we, for example, plan to industrialize Iran. These economic safeguards will prevent the society from regressing to a class society. The amount and kind of production will be determined by general consumption and the needs of the people of the country. We will only produce items which are to be consumed by all, and are necessary items of consumption.

We will check consumption against the five principles and we will find out which items do not need to be consumed by the society. Anything which sets one individual above others, whether in the way of food or clothing, is forbidden and must not be produced. Production has fallen on the wrong course and has created great deprivation. Privation has reached such a degree for the great masses of humanity that they suffer from hunger. They have neither jobs nor bread to eat. Why?

Because a few want to wear expensive, imported ties or clothing made of "Fantasy Fabrics," to build million-dollar palaces or ride in such-and-such model automobile.

The universities will be based on the same idea. There, we will not train masters to ride the people, as is done in the present university system. In Iran, universities were created merely to fill government offices. But, we want to train spiritual leaders in a state of constant uprising, just and monotheistic. Such is our goal. We will not confine science within the framework of the expectation of domination, but we will harmonize it with the expectations of Monotheistic Unity. Hence, in technology, we will follow fields which would make possible the satisfaction of the needs of the society. For example, if we establish a textile factory, the products will be based on the regional climates of Iran, because the natural use of fabric is to protect people from cold and heat and not to make a human being alienated from himself. The material produced will satisfy the needs of human beings in their natural environment. In other words, industrial choices will be based on the needs of human beings moving on the course to freedom.

In planning, the goals of programs will be determined through elections. In economic planning, in production and consumption, the fundamental principles will be our guide. Hence, in textile factories, for example, we will only take into account the natural environment, and the product must change the face of society in such a way as to ensure the manifestation of Monotheistic Unity. That is why Islam discourages the individual from wearing clothing which would set him apart from others.

Therefore, the goal of production is not more and more consumption. When the basis of production is Monotheistic Unity, the consumption system must also follow the principle of Monotheistic Unity. For example in the transportation industry, since our basis is Monotheistic Unity, we must have a technology and production method which would provide us with public transportation. In this way, we will prevent great consumption and waste, which the West itself does not know how to deal with.

Malthus has said that the human population will increase such that a day will come when people on earth will not even have the space to stand up and they will be forced to eat each other. Even if this prediction has not come true concerning human beings, it is now true concerning automobiles. In the streets, they are stuck to each other so tightly that they have to devour each other. And for what?

In order to prevent a crisis in the system, the surplus income of economic production must be utilized to refuel the society. We want to employ it in ways which will create movement (the principle of Spiritual Mission). Thus, an Islamic government will follow a production system which would respond to the most basic human needs within the framework of freedom. You will see that it is only Islam which can respond to these needs. No other system has been able to respond from every direction to the question of human freedom. This is not to make Islam out to be an absolute. This is merely an expression of reality. The value system dominating consumption in the West has also spread to Russia. You can see what direction it has given to production in that country.

In any case, in economics, we cannot accept a method of production that is appropriate to a class society, a dualistic society. In this area, too, we will act on the basis of Monotheistic Unity. hence, in consumption also, we must follow our religious mandates.

Take, for example, the Western suit we wear. This suit carries with it a code of behavior. It is not suitable for sitting on the ground; it requires ironing, and it requires a chair. As soon as you change the form of your clothing, your house must also change your family room must change, your living room must change. Now, suppose all of these have changed. In Iran, where are you to get the things from? They must come from the West. In this way, the West spreads certain values throughout Iran and forcefully creates a market for its products. But, we do not want this. We want to bring consumption to a level where it can make human beings free, not captive. At the present time, the human being has become a slave to consumption. We want him to become free from it. We want him to only consume things which will free him. For example, we regard hunger as slaverly; when a person becomes hungry, he has nothing else, and his intellect stops functioning. Well, you must first feed him; you must cure his hunger. But how?

Those who are experts in these fields and who want to establish an Islamic government have a duty to study these problems. If we are to plan certain programs there in Iran, we must know what in the way of food may be produced in that land, given that climate. Note here: not in the climate of the West, but in the climate of Iran! What items can we produce to be able to supply everyone with the necessary calories, etc.? This will form our production program. Other than this, we will not produce.

Concerning housing, the different regions of Iran have been divided into earthquake zones. In every one of the habitable regions of Iran, there is a probability of a deadly, devastating earthquake every three years, on the average. Well, a country such as this, with such an unstable nature, requires study. There are several ways to solve the problem. In the present system, they say that those who can should make sturdy houses which would withstand earthquakes and those who cannot afford it should remain in their huts to be destroyed with one tremble of the ground. Well, this problem must be studied. We do not intend to build palaces for a few and ruins for the rest.

Our principle is Monotheistic Unity, and we must walk along the path of Justice. Therefore, houses must be built with the duty in mind of lodging each family in a way that is appropriate to a free life and that will not make him captive.

Islamic architecture is free of the expectations of dominators. It intends neither to fill the pockets of one person or another, nor to give the opportunity to the ruling power to bridle and control the society, nor to pollute the atmosphere with sex, etc. A house should not be built to become a storehouse for the products of indsutrial factories, which do not satisfy any basic need. Such things do not occur in Islamic architecture. A house must answer the human need for freedom.

The guiding principles are always those fundamental principles. Freedom from the domination of nature and social domination will be the essential bases for the production-consumption system, so that the very appearance of an Iranian city or village would, at a glance, clearly reveal that it is a center of Monotheistic Unity. At the dawn of Islam, when Moslems became dominant over others and wealth began to flow towards Arabia, the wealthy built large houses with several stories. Omar realized that he had taken a wrong turn. He said, "If I live another year, I will have those extra stories which stand out above the others destroyed so that all the houses manifest Monotheistic Unity."

The technique of Islamic architecture is different from that which is taught today. The architecture of today is part of a class society; it is designed to enslave human beings, to create consumer markets. When you visit a Western house, you can see that this architecture has created a felt need for many unnecessary items. In Islam, the production system determines and regulates the consumer item. In other words, it makes the house conform to the kind of clothes you wear, the food you eat, your relations with others, and other human needs, because in all of this, our principles are Monotheistic Unity, Continual spiritual Mission, Spiritual Leadership, Justice, and the ultimate society of Monotheistic Unity. In technology, agriculture, and so on, we will take all of these principles into consideration.

Hence, the third safeguard prevents the political power and leadership in the society from becoming the dominant power and directs the society toward Monotheistic Unity, wherein an economy based on autocracy and dualism no longer exists. You can see that an all-encompassing program is possible, based on these five principls. You see that we can deal with our problems within a theoretical framework as a thought system, a system for the recognition of truth, a system for investigating the future, a system for directing movement. In a manifesto, we can put all these ideas at everyone's disposal and set ourselves up as a practical manifestation of that manifesto for the society to see and evaluate. This is more important than anything else, because as long as the society does not see in us, at the present time, the values dominating the society of the future, it will not be set in motion. Everybody talks pretty talk; it is pretty action which no one engages in. And actions speak louder than words.

We must make the principle of future Spiritual Leadership a matter of the present in ourselves. In 'Ali, we can see the whole of mankind's future history; in him we can see the ultimate future of mankind. That is why he is a spiritual leader. Otherwise, he physically died fourteen centuries ago. Spiritual Leadership was not part of his body, it was in his actions, actions which still remain the example, the model, the proof of a spiritual leader.

Let me repeat: We must make the future a matter of the present in our own beings. This is the meaning of a spiritual leader. We must be the expressers of Monotheistic Unity and.

the expressions of the Islamic system; that is, we must move on the path of Justice, noting carefully what the greatest victory of a revolution consists of. First of all, those who want to make a revolution must believe in themselves as transformers. This is 'Ali's saying, a great, revolutinary saying. In conformity with the five fundamental principles, we must first have faith in ourselves, but not make gods and absolutes of ourselves. This would indicate lack of faith in ourselves. We must avoid rationalizations.

Believing in ourselves means believing: My brain and body are able, if I put them to work. Any brain which is destroyed, mine can replace, and any gun dropped on the ground, my hand is capable of retrieving. If my brain is set to work, my hand will take up the gun and our movement, our struggle, and God's party will be victorious. The second condition is that the revolutionary must be in and of himself an expression of the society of tomorrow. He must be an illustration of the free society of Monotheistic Unity.

I hope you do not think that what has been said here needs no alteration, interpretation, or clarification. You, too, must think about these issues and help to clarify the ambiguities, so that in our future talks, we can provide the essential lines for the manifesto of an Islamic government in today's world on the basis of the actual recognition of exisiting relationships and set ourselves, our society, and our world in motion.

And for God's promise to materialize, "Indeed, the people of God are victorious." We can be part of God's party, and we can be victorious.

NOTES

1. Reference to the occupation of Iran by the Allied forces despite Iran's declared neutrality.

2. *Not in a general, compulsory army which takes the youth, holds them in barracks, and then kills their parents, brothers, and sisters in June of 1963.*[3]

3. See note 1 in Chapter 1.

ADDENDUM

Editor's Note. In the closing stages of the preparation of this volume it was learned that Mr. Abolhassan Banisadr has been removed from the positions of president and commander-in-chief of the armed forces by the Ayatollah Khomeini. Khomeini's action culminated the end of an apparent power struggle that had been going on in Iran between Banisadr and the fundamentalists belonging to the Islamic Republic Party. Several weeks later, Banisadr entered France seeking political asylum.

Shortly after his arrival in France, Banisadr issued a proclamation, "A Covenant" *(Misaq)*, announcing the formation of the Council for the National Resistance Front with Mr. Mas'od Rajavi, one of the leaders of the People's *Mojahedin* Organization, as its leader. The twelve-page typewritten document contains several historically and politically significant points about the government of the Islamic Republic of Iran and Banisadr's own involvement in the establishment of that government. The inclusion of a translation of this document here is meant to provide readers with an up-dating of Banisadr's theoretical ideas as well as a wider perspective of him as a practitioner of those ideas. Notes appearing at the end are those of the editor's.

A COVENANT
of the Council for the National Resistance Front*

People of Iran, women, men, political groups and parties who support independence, freedom, and an Islamic republic: When the last blows were inflicted on what remained of freedom and I saw the claimers of the rule paving the way to dependency, I rejected the last message of Mr. Khomeini which was handed to me in Kermanshah. He had said that if I did not protest the elimination of all freedom, would compromise with the governing gang, and approve of the overtaking of the institutions of law, such as the Judicial Council, the Council of Guardians, the Parliament, the Cabinet, the newspapers, and radio and television, I would be allowed to keep the positions of president and commander-in-chief of the armed forces; otherwise, he would go to any lengths (even threatening arrest and execution). My efforts of seventeen months to make understood that titles such as president and commander-in-chief of the armed forces are important only if

89

they serve the goals of the revolution, which are based on independence and freedom, were not heeded. He imagined, and still does, that these positions are intrinsically valuable and that to hold on to them, a man of principle would be willing to sacrifice those goals. How could those who have done so themselves believe otherwise? In any case, when independence were destroyed, when the present regime rapidly took on the characteristics of the previous one, and when there remained no room for doubt that the United States, with its multifaceted influence, was destroying the true opponents of the establishment of their desired regime at the hands of the present rulers, as a responsible person elected and trusted by you, the people, I determined to put up resistance, to put together this covenant to save the revolution and preserve those principles which had been embraced before the revolution and which were eliminated in the course of two and a half years, and to ask everyone to join in, endorse it, and wholeheartedly attempt to bring about its materialization, confident that when the will not to surrender for the victory is created in them, victory will already have been achieved. Before the victory of the revolution, signals given by the enemy indicated that U.S. policy was based on the establishment of a stable regime in Iran. According to this policy, the desirable stable regime would have two main characteristics:

A. The people of the country would submit to it as necessary and inevitable. In other words, the active social forces opposing U.S. policy should be eliminated and the social atmosphere for them should not develop.

B. The structures of dependency should be preserved and consolidated. The implementation of this policy would depend firstly on the materialization of the U.S. motto: neither the shah as the symbol of the consolidated ruling forces, nor Khomeini as the expression of the forces opposing U.S. policy.

The case with the shah was clear, but Khomeini could not be eliminated as the people's source of emulation except through a religio-political metamorphosis establishing a regime desirable to the United States. This was clear to me from the start and, therefore, in the analyses that I regularly prepared for him, I emphasized this fact. What could only be theoretically arrived at then is now—when the regime is two and a half years old—obvious to everyone:

(a) Not only has this regime failed to reduce dependency,

it has added to it both qualitatively and quantitatively. For instance, the budget ratified for the current year indicates complete dependency.

(b) Such changes have taken place regarding Islam and its freedoms, that the previous regime of the shah has become desirable! Now, the regime is engaged in eliminating the politico-social obstacles, the political forces which oppose the establishment of a regime desirable to the United States. I had frequently warned that the eliminators will be eliminated in accordance with the law of elimination. But power, in the course of its consolidation, forces its rules upon the weak enforcers. If we want to find out which among he personalities and political ideologies have gone astray, it would be sufficient to bring to mind once again those principles which were espoused in Paris by Mr. Khomeini and which I was actively involved in formulating, principles which I considered obstacles for the United States to achieve its objectives, in order to see who and what groups have ignored them and are practically serving U.S. policy.

(i) The first principle upon which the Islamic government was to be based was that of independence — political, economic, cultural, and, consequently, social independence, the change in the social structure of society to eliminate the advantaged stata and groups who exist as a result of dependency.

It should be remembered that the advisors to Mr. Khomeini within the country were pointing out that the shah's regime would fall if he did not attack the United States. Hence, from the start, there were two lines of thought, that of those who would not in the least want to see the United States go and that of those who saw the shah's regime at a dead end and believed that a dependent Iran would not only fail to develop but could not even survive. What has happened to the revolution leaves no room for doubt that those who sought to come to an understanding with the United States (or to strengthen dependency by pretending to oppose the United States) have dominated the leadership of the revolution. Today, everyone knows that the Americans approached everyone. It is known who accepted a compromise and who did not. A statement I consistently made to Mr. Khomeini was: the people consider you a religious source of emulation and not a politician specialized in internal and external relations. It is most unfortunate that he did not heed this statement and has done to

91

Islam, the country, and his own personality what he has done and still does.

In any case, our effort is to save the Iranian revolution. The revolutionary effort to obstruct the way for American policy to establish a dependent stable regime must begin with the principle of independence and the acceptance of an all-encompassing program in order to achieve it. Only those political and ideological forces should be allowed to participate who believe wholeheartedly in independence, that is, those who refuse the domination of any foreign superpower in any political, economic, or cultural area and in domestic political activities, would not by any means bring in foreign powers. Not only the experience of our revolution but also that of the last half century in other countries clarifies for us the reality that when instead of a program of independence being implemented, foreign policy is used as a weapon to seize monopolistic power and to oust those who protest such a policy, sooner or later negative use (suppressing opponents for having such a policy) will be replaced with positive use, that is, wheeling and dealing with that policy.

(ii.) Freedom as a reflection of independence in foreign policy was accepted as the second principle of an Islamic republic. In Paris, under the banner of freedom and in its interpretation, the following principles were declared by Mr. Khomeini dozens of times; they were expressed in interviews and were published throughout the world; in fact, they became for our people, the intellectuals, and political forces a covenant with the leadership:

1. Freedom of expression and the abolition of any kind of censorship. At that time, Islam was not considered a religion for the government by one group. There was no talk of dictatorship or even of religious guardian jurisprudence (*velayat-e faqih*).[1] With condifence in the truth of Islam and the reliance of this religion on knowledge, we considered essential the abolition of all forms of consorship to create the atmosphere for the manifestation of Islam as a methodology for development. We said that Islam, with its understanding of the relationship between the material and the spiritual, is the way out for contemporary societies in crisis and those who suffer from crises will not become aware of this reality unless censorship—all censorship—is abolished and complete freedom of expression governs. Today you are all witness to the state of this

freedom. You all witness that the youth, even the children, are considered rebellious and are executed for shouting slogans or distributing leaflets and newspapers.

Here, I must add that Mr. Gilani has given me one month to go to Mr. Khomeini and repent. Regardless of the fact that one should only repent to God—and I will not ask for which sins I should repent—I am prepared to repent of all the sins I have or have not committed provided that Mr. Khomeini becomes the same Mr. Khomeini of Paris and wants, implements, and is bound to the same Islam that he espoused in Paris. In any case, reinstigating the revolution and redirecting it to its original path will not be possible without adhering to freedoms such as the freedcom of expression, meaning the abolition of all censorship. We must not forget that if we do not want to have one or even several groups run the country who would enforce their own ideology (which would necessitate the interference of foreign powers and dependency), we will have to rely on the awareness, the growth, and the conscience of the public and the promotion of their understanding. With censorship, this is impossible. Today, the business of considering the people as sheep has reached such a level that he wants 15 million votes for the presidential elections. But this 15 million, who must give their votes under all kinds of religious and other pressures, do not need to know why they should vote, who they are voting for, and for what program they are voting. Is the situation not worse than that of the shah's regime? *We have witnessed the downfall of that regime, the downfall of Khomeini's regime, as well, has long been obvious to everyone. If we want to close the way to the agents of the United States and be able to live in this world independently, there is no other way than to promote public awareness. And this will not take place without the abolition of censorship.*[2]

2. The abolition of ideological persecution. In Paris, it seemed clear to Mr. Khomeini that in this world, the interaction of ideas and views cannot be restricted, let alone eliminated. Therefore, the way to defend Islam is not, by any means, through the courts of revolution, torture, etc. When we said that we would not have political prisoners in the Islamic republic, he himself frequently said that the shah's regime had built prisons instead of anything else. With his coming to Iran and the cration of the Revolutionary Court, it became obvious to me that this Court would in the end become an organization

93

for the censorship of ideas and a butchery of brains. That is why from the very beginning I opposed it and its operations, saying that the main figures of the shah's regime must be tried in regular courts in order both to establish from the very beginning respect for the human being and the rule of law and also to make known to today's generation through open trials all the truths about the previous regime, especially the truth of the absolute rule by the United States over the destiny of its country. And this second reason is the more important. I protested against this Court and its operations again and again in the Revolutionary Council. I spoke to Mr. Khomeini many times objecting to it and I have written many letters in this regard, all of which are available. In the early months of the presidency, it was decided that these courts should be abolished, but gradually, political power became more centralized and more attention was given to them as a means to eliminate the new political opponents. It has reached such a state today that they have destroyed any sort of political, intellectual, professional, and other safeguards. Based on these facts, to redirect the revolution to its main course and, as the basic step, to prevent the establishment of a regime dependent on the West, there is no other way than to accept the aspects of freedom and to safeguard their implementation. In our republic, there shall exist no political crime for believing in one ideology or another and we will have no prisons and no prisoners in this regard.

No execution or any kind of punishment shall exist for having an ideology. All those who have committed crimes for political reasons—even the killing of children—during the previous shah's regime or the present regime will be tried in regular, open courts.

3. In Paris, it was not only accepted that anyone with any ideology would have the right to express his opinion, but it was also accepted that he would have the right to oppose the ideology of the government. Freedom of *fatva*, a religious proclamation, was also accepted and no one could have imagined that they would execute children, youths, and bazaar merchants for having participated in demonstrations which had been prohibited by the "Guardian."[3]

I will not involve myself in the discussion of whether or not such things exist in Islam. I will not deal with the issue that one of the aspects of Greekstruckness (historical Weststruckness) is the statement that justice is to be administered in accordance with the will of the ruler.[4] I say that our understanding of the temporal and spatial situation of our own society was that using the weapon of the "accusation of heresy" and damaging the principle of the involvement of the public in the affairs of the government sacrifice Islam and weaken it in solving the problems and difficulties of today's society which wants to free itself through revolution. Mr. Khomeini, who had accepted this concept and who had expressed it many times, could not, despite all his efforts, prevent this concept from becoming a principle in the Constitution. Therefore, what the Revolutionary Courts are doing is contrary to the Constitution and contrary to the positions decided on in Paris. For many reasons, the actions of those elements influenced by American policy in the present ruling circles will cause the destruction of Islam. Therefore, returning to the concepts and values upon which the revolution materialized depends on: no party, group, or persnality having the monopolistic right of decision making or proclamations and the expression of decisions and freedom of divine science [ejtehad] being sacred, universal rights.

Opposition to decisions, religious proclamations, and even the law (if it does not obstruct the implementation of the law) are the rights of parties, groups, and individuals and no one can deprive them of this right. The method which has been used and is being used in a religious dictatorship, Stalinism, or fascism, would be considered a crime in the republic. Not only should the executive branch not be allowed to consider individuals rebellious merely for their opposition, gatherings, or any other kind of constructive opposition, but it should be duty-bound to provide the means for the expression of opposing views.

Of course, the freedoms are not confined to those mentioned above. Many other freedoms were espoused by him in Paris (such as the freedom of dress for men and women, freedom of education, cultural freedom for various ethnic groups, freedom of religious practices for various religious groups), which have all been trampled today. These freedoms have all been trampled in the name of Islam and their violation is one of the blows inflicted on Islam. The restitution of all these freedoms is absolutely necessary for the construction of a monotheistically unified [towhidi] society.[5] We insist emphatically on the above-mentioned freedoms because we know that other freedoms will be trampled and that economic and cultural inequalities and all sorts of dependencies are all calamities which will be inflicted on our society with the elimination of these freedoms.

(iii) In Paris, in the political arena, it was accepted that in Islam it is not the individual who governs but the law. Based on this, it was considered obvious that if the implementation of Islamic law were safeguarded, the government of individuals merely because they belong to a special stratum would be unnecessary. Hence, he himself stated clearly that when he went to Iran, he would return to Qom, do his own work, and would only oversee affairs.[6] In Paris, I told Mr. Habibi to prepare a Constitution, which he started. He would take it to him part by part, discuss it with him, and obtain his approval. That text was also studied in Qom by the scholars and teachers of the Center and later, with twice revisions, it became the rough draft. He himself, as well as other scholars, saw the rough draft. He had certain criticisms which he had written himself in his own hand, which are available. Mr. Beheshti and I went to him in Qom and eliminated in person all of his nine objections, except the one concerning the president of the republic not being a woman.[7] It was settled that this issue should be studied in the Assembly of Experts. Before the formation of the Assembly of Experts, there was no talk of religious guardian jurisprudence, let alone religious dectatorial jurisprudence. Again, I do not want to raise the issue of at least 90 percent of Shi'i religious scholars being opposed to religious government [velayat] meaning the political government of an individual. This, too, is one of the signs of Greekstruckness, which is the direct influence of the Christian Church. I believe that in this world, enforcing religious government is impossible except through public vote, which depends upon the growth of the society, and, as we are witnessing, ends in the dictatorship of the clergy. Today's behavior of Mr. Khomeini — when he prohibits the expression of views by other sources of emulation and when masses of children and young people are executed for their opposition to the "just religious jurist" — is not only a diviation on his part from the statements he made in Paris, which are reflected in the text of the Constitution which was prepared under his own supervision, and a deviation from the present Constitution, which determines the limitations of his duties and authority, but it will also cause discredit to Islam and will inflict the harshest blow upon it. The result of this kind of religious guardian jurisprudence, which is worse than the worst of dictatorships, is the situation the country is found in now: hostage taking and its economic consequences (a minimum of $80 billion in damages as a result of the economic embargo and the war) and internal and external wars have no cause other than his dictatorial decisions and the advantages taken of his weakness by the power hungry group. J we note the condition that Islam is found in for the younger generation of the country and the people of the world, we realize more clearly the danger of individual autocracy (wherther religious, monarchical, ideological, ethnical, etc.). Redirecting the revolution on its own course will not only depend on putting an end to this type of dictatorial guardianship but (because similar to this "guardianship" would be that of those parties who establish dictatorships after victory) will necessitate the prohibition of the dictatorial guardianship of parties, groups, etc. In this republic — as the abolition of dictatorship was accepted in the course of the Islamic revolution and since the Constitutional Revolution — any kind of guardianship can only be implemented through a public vote and the free will of the people of the country.

(iv) In Paris, the principle of criticism was accepted and Mr. Khomeini sought criticism of himself by others. It was the expression of freedom in Islam. In Tehran, following the speech on *Ashura* and in Hoseyniyyeh Ershad, he told me: Your intention by your statement that we have only fourteen infallibly perfect ones [*ma'sum*] and the fourteenth one is in occultation is to prove that I (meaning him) am faulty and make mistakes.[8] Of course, this suspicion had been suggested to him and I had no such intention. But a detailed study of all the views formed concerning the government and noting the consequences of considering a personality infallibly perfect in Iran (whether during the previous regime or in the present regime, in which, according to Mr. Mohammad Gilani,[9] Mr. Khomeini is considered infallibly perfect and anyone opposing him would be considered a sinner deserving of execution), or the party in the Soviet Union and similar countries, will leave no room for doubt that the *Shi'ahs* are right to consider the infallibly perfect one in occultation, in order to establish the principle that the individual, group, party, front, or ruler can be criticized.

Therefore, rechanneling the revolution to its original course would mean not recognizing an individual, group, party, or anything else as infallibly perfect. The conclusion is that criticism (in the true sense of the word) of the leadership is the right of the people and they must be encouraged to exercise it.

(v) Historical experience tells us that the only successful political method is to combine all political leanings into one united front. This was not only accepted by Mr. Khomeini, but he himself more than anyone else would emphasize and insist that "parties, groups, etc. should forget their seasonal disputes and become united." In Paris, too, he was of the same opinion. But as he was making a revolution from Najaf to Paris, since his return to Tehran, he has been making a counterrevolution. He has abandoned the realistic revolutionary political path and gradually begun to favor eliminationary political path and gradually begun to favor elimination. And today, he is determined to even eliminate groups with Islamic leanings who do not conform to his dictatorship. The former shah, too, from his White Revolution onward, even in dealing with ideological leanings which were loyal to his regime, gradually made elimination the foundation and he ended up the way we have witnessed. This great affliciton of our revolution has also been the great affliction of other revolutions, which is why we must rapidly return to the accepted principles if we want to save the revolution from downfall.

In this republic, no personality, no group, nothing will enjoy "hegemonical" priority and none will have the right to eliminate others.

Leaning towards the creation of a political front will be regarded as the main leaning and all ideologies, groups, and parties who believe in independence, freedom, and an Islamic republic are bound to make an effort to create this front. Those groups who are prepared to participate in this front must immediately form it. Even if only one group is prepared for action, it must act as the representative of one front and must make every effort to bring others in.

(vi) In Paris, many other political lines were also accepted and Mr. Khomeini was ahead of everyone.

In an interview, he said that a woman could not only become a representative or a minister, but even president. In Tehran, I reminded him of this statement. He responded: There, I made certain expedient statements; but I do not feel bound by them. (In the Assembly of Founders and in the presence of members of the Revolutionary Council, including Mr. Bazargan, he made a similar statement concerning that assembly.) Again, I pointed out to him: The people recognize you as a source of emulation, consider your statements religious decrees, and base their actions upon them. In the course of Iranian history, it has always been said that the king must not make contradictory statements, let alone the religious source of emulation. Which statement should the people consider a religious expression, the one of yesterday, today, or tomorrow? In any case, in this republic, we must return to those positions of Paris and accept that in an Islamic society, growth will not occur unless women can attain their full potential in all aspects and are given appropriate political, economic, and cultural rights. Concerning the various ethnic groups which form our nation, the situation should be the same. Within the boundaries of independence, territorial integrity, and unity of the country, all ethnic groups should enjoy equal rights and the management of local affairs should belong to them based on the institution of councils.

(vii) In the political administration of the society, another principle which was the policy and which was abandoned was that of councils. In the early days of the revolution, certain efforts were made to create councils in the various political, economic, and cultural domains to be employed as a method of administration and leadership. But, they did not last, because of the tendency towards individual and group autocracy and they were abandoned. Not only did the political leadership of the country not find them harmonious with its dictatorial rule but in addition, the organized councils themselves became means either to enforce the policies of the political groups or to establish the dictatorship of the members of the councils. Now, if we want the administration to be based on a system of councils, we can do nothing but to implement carefully and decisively the principles which were mentioned earlier.

(viii) One of the political principles which was accepted, even emphatically, by Mr. Khomeini from 1961 until the rejection and banishment of the nationalists became the policy was that Moslem and Iranian were considered as two sides of a coin. In his last interview before he left Najaf, he considered the establishment of a national government as the basic step in establishing an Islamic government. It was unquestionably accepted that Iran was a nation with a historical culture and a country which has the right to exist independently. Not only did he find no conflict between being Moslem and Iranian, he did not even consider them a duality. I myself, in one of the analytical reports I prepared for him, described the fact that it is the historical experience throughout the world, including Iran, that the condition for victory in every revolution depends on the materialization of the following three social needs:

The need for a nationality, which necessitates putting an end to internal disunity and dispersion, as well as independence from other countries; the need for social reforms, which necessitates fundamental change in social relationships to rescue the deprived of the society; and the need for spirituality, religion, or ideology as the expression of the above needs as well as the human need for freedom and growth in historical contunuity.

Now, these needs have been suppressed and redirecting the revolution on its own course depends, among other things, on returning to the principle of the inseparability of being Moslem and Iranian. Other principles, including the principle of elections, which would depend on the freedom of voting; the principle of a government of competence and principles instead of a government of relationships, which was the old way in the country; and the principle of eliminating personal relationships in power, which has, unfortunately, been revived and is worse than it was during the time of the shah (look at the makeup of the Parliament, the government, and the new rulers and consider their relationships with one another), are all principles that must be put into action. If the above principles are carried out, these principles will naturally follow.

(ix) Although it is clear that the implementation of the above principles and a complete program of independence would require a new economic system, the need for a change in the economic system must be emphasized. The need for this change was accepted in Paris. A few years before the revolution, I arrived at the conclusion, through methological research, that the shah's regime had reached a dead end and was going to fall. I compiled the results of fifteen years of research on the problems of Iran into the problems of the country and their solutions and gave them to Mr. Khomeini in Najaf to study. The response from Najaf was that I should publish this proclamation (the same proclamation of the Islamic Republic of Iran or the program for political, economic, cultural, and social independence). And in the early months of the revolution, an effort was made to sever economic dependencies and change the economic structure of the country. But like the rest of affairs, it was forestalled. Now, in order to return the revolution to its original course, the principle of an Islamic economic system to eliminate any kind of economic domination of one group over another and provide an opportunity for the equal growth of the individuals of the society is of vital importance. Since I have explained the components of this principle in *Eqtesad-e Towhidi* [*Towhidi* Economics] and in the proclamation, I will not go into detail here.

(x) In the domain of culture, cultural independence and escape from historical Weststruckness (Greekstruckness), modern Weststruckness, and the creation of the background for the appearance of new creative, responsible, experienced, and teachable human beings are necessities which cannot be ignored. The greatest of deviations is the deviation from the domain of culture. The spirituality which brought the revolution to victory and became victorious with the revolution was violently driven off the state by the rule of low, backward materialism. Under the banner of fighting Weststruckness, cultural stagnation and congelation became the basis and in this age of lightning changes, the ground was prepared for the worst kind of dependency. In having emphasis placed on appearances, brains and expertise have been humiliated and driven away.

Returning the revolution to its own course would not only mean extending the resources and the institutions of learning, but also would mean providing a free atmosphere for thought and actions so that a Moslem human being can present through innovation a new culture which is the expression of the general wishes of all the deprived and downtrodden in the world.

(xi) Parallel to and acompanying the above principles should be the social changes for the attainment of a monotheistically unified society. It is quite clear that such a society will be monotheistically unified because in it relationships are not based on force and, therefore, the construction of such a society will be possible. My experience since the revolution and in the positions of president and commander-in-chief of the armed forces leaves me with no doubt that rapid and desirable changes in the area of independence are possible provided that we not consider force as our means. I have devised the above principles on this very basis. I believe that only those groups and individuals can be united to act as pioneers of the revolution who would accept this covenant and sincerely attempt to materialize it. But these principles in action require a complete program to bring about overall independence. The proclamation of the Islamic republic which has been prepared considering the realities of the country — and these realities are the same as they were — is a program for political and economic independence and fundamental social changes to preserve independence and move towards a *towhidi* society. This program has been discussed inside and outside the country since 1972 by people with varying ideologies and has been continually approved by them. Alas, the tendency to establish a dictatorship and the various domestic and foreign conspiracies did not allow a chance for its implementation. How could this program be carried out when not only would its implementation require the implementation of those principles I have recounted, but this program would negate the system that they wanted and want and that they were and are establishing. I believe that the main duty of every faithful human being is to close the way to the overall redomination of the United States sand the influence of any other foreign power (the Soviet Union, Europe, China, etc.). By considering these principles and the influence of any other foreign power (the Soviet Union, nation must rise up to put these principles into action and put an end to the rule of all sorts of bludgeons, censorship etc. — in a word, all sorts of force.

I had not planned to remain and resist, but when I determined that these deviations and what is being done are, first of all, attempting to eliminate the main forces which oppose the domination of the United States over the country, which will then end in the establishment of a stable and lasting rule by the United States through the counterrevolutionary factions, I determined to stay and try my best to save the revolution, religion, and my country.

The great nation of Iran urgently demands resistance by me, by all the political groups and parties, and by all the factions and individuals who are prepared, despite all inherent dangers, to aid in this great effort and who would sacrifice their lives to bring victory to the revolution. Despite the situation which they have created by deviating from the demands and positions of the revolution, and despite the unmatched atmosphere of suppression, fear, and terror which they have brought about, I believe in the abilities of the younger generation of the country and I am certain that this able and active generation will eliminate the obstacles and become victorious.

The Elected President of the People of Iran
Abolhassan Banisadr
July 18, 1981

*Translated from the original Persian text by Mohammad R. Ghanoonparvar.
Translation Copyright© 1981 by Mazda Publishers.

NOTES

1. The concept of *velayat-e faqih,* or the rule of the religious jurisprudent, has been the subject of a book by Khomeini entitled *Islamic Government* in which he attempts to lay the foundation of an Islamic form of government based upon his *own* interpretation of the Islamic law and the *Shi'i* doctrine. The *faqih* is defined as a man possessing two qualifications: He is knowledgeable in the Islamic law, and is a just person. If such a man could be found capable of forming a government, then "it is everyone's duty to obey him." See *Islamic Government,* third printing, 1971, p. 63, (In Persian).

2. Emphasis is that of Banisadr's.

3. Reference to Ayatollah Khomeini.

4. See note 2, page xiv.

5. See note 1, page xiv.

6. Qom: a city to the south of Tehran is the center of Iranian *Shi'i* theological learning and is where most of the high-ranking ayatollahs live and teach.

7. Ayatollah Mohammad Beheshti, killed in the bombing of the headquarters of the Islamic Republic Party (IRP) in June, 1981, was one of the founders of the IRP and a close associate and a former student of Khomeini. By some accounts he was the second most powerful man in Iran at the time of his death.

8. *Ashura:* the day when Imam Hossein, the third imam of the *Shi'ahs,* was killed in a battle against Yazid (son of Mo'aviyeh the founder of Umayyed dynasty). His death and the circumstances surrounding it have evolved through out *Shi'i* history into a symbol of resistance against tyranny and despotism.

   On Hoseyniyyeh Ershad, see note 26, page 56.

   ma'sum: Reference to the household of Prophet Mahammad and the twelve imams whom *Shi'ahs* believe to be infalliably perfect and devoid of all sin.

9. Ayatollah Mohammad Gilani is the chief prosecutor of the Islamic Revolutionary Court and a staunch supporter of Khomeini.

Available NOW!

Iran: Essays on a Revolution in the
Making, edited by Ahmad Jabbari and
Robert Olson, (1981), 214, paper.
$4.95. ISBN: 0-939214-00-8.

Contents:

Thomas Ricks: Background to the Iranian Revolution: Imperialism,
Dictatorship, and Nationalism, 1872 to 1979;
G. Hossein Razi: Development of Political Institutions in Iran and
Scenarios for the Future;
Soheyl Amini: A Critical Assessment of 'Ali Shari'ati's Theory of
Revolution;
Shahin E. Tabatabai: Women in Islam;
Michael C. Hillmann: Revolution, Islam, and Contemporary Per-
sian Literature;
Allan N. Williams: Revolutionary Struggle over Economy: Some Ex-
perienced Bench Marks;
Ahmad Jabbari: Economic Factors in Iran's Revolution: Poverty,
Inequality, and Inflation.

Forthcoming. . .
Iranian Society: An Anthology of Writings by Jalal Al-e Ahmad,
compiled and edited by Michael C. Hillmann.

Works in Progress. . .
*A Man of Law and Peace: The Biography of Dr. Moham-
mad Mosaddeq,* by Ahmad Jabbari;

*Ayattolah Khomeini Speaks: A Critical Analysis of Khomeini's
Historical Speeches and Proclamations, 1963 to 1981,*
translated and edited by Ahmad Jabbari and Soheyl Amini.

In Translation. . .

Islam and Ownership, by Seyyed Mahmood *"Father"*
Taleqani.